Elsa's Own Blue Zone

By Sharon Textor-Black

New York

Elsa's Own Blue Zone

America's Centenarian Sweetheart's Insights for Positive Aging and Living

ISBN 978-1-60037-579-8

Library of Congress Control Number: 2009921175

MORGAN · JAMES
THE ENTREPRENEURIAL PUBLISHER

Morgan James Publishing, LLC
1225 Franklin Ave., STE 325
Garden City, NY 11530-1693
Toll Free 800-485-4943
www.MorganJamesPublishing.com

About the Cover

Taken at a fashion show charity event for QUOTA International, Elsa holds tightly to her raffle tickets as volunteer greeter and model escort Paul Jasinto sweeps Elsa off her feet.

The QUOTA organization helps disadvantaged and abused women, as well as the deaf, in 14 countries. This event was held at the Fort Lauderdale Marriott in 2008. Elsa is seen here at age 100.

Paul Jasinto, the gentleman holding Elsa on the front cover, hails from Miramar, Florida. He is a chemistry major at Carnegie Mellon University, Pittsburgh, PA, class of 2012. Paul is a fine young man, who in our brief time knowing him, has demonstrated several of Elsa's insights. He volunteered his time for others at the QUOTA fundraiser where this photo was taken. He showed "No Fear" by being brave enough to enhance the event with his fun costume. Paul showed enthusiasm and respect for Elsa and her inspiring example. In addition, his sincere smile is priceless.

Kudos to Paul's family for bringing up such a terrific guy ... and also to Carnegie Mellon for accepting such a well-rounded individual with such obvious character and great promise into their program.

Dedication

It is with great love that I appreciate and thank my husband Mike for his support and patience. He often covered for me at work and at home with our children during this project, and did so without complaint. Mike has a heart of gold.

I also dedicate this book to my mom who is also my indispensible business associate, Joan Marie Hoffmann Textor. She always helped to bring me back up when balancing it all seemed insurmountable. We all need a Joan in our lives!

Contents

Testimonials

"I'm a big believer that we need heroes and role models—especially role models to show us how to live well into our hundreds. When I interviewed Elsa Hoffmann by phone for my podcast, *Ageless Lifestyles*, I was impressed with how she listened and answered the questions I asked as opposed to rehearsed questions or whatever was on her mind. She instantly became one of my heroes. You cannot find a better role model of a vital, life embracing centenarian. What does she model? She loves life and loves people. Her greatest joy is making others happy and helping people connect with other people and enjoy themselves. She is cheerful, friendly and primarily focused on the present. She isn't afraid to live alone, drive, or tackle technology like her cell phone. Hardly a prima donna who has others taking care of her, on the day I called she had been busy ironing. The only reason it might be hard to meet her is that you have to catch her—she's always off to one event to another. She knows to prime the pump by exercising, meditating, and getting enough rest. She knows not to dwell on problems but to either deal with a problem or let it go. When I asked her about the greatest adversities in her life, she had a hard time coming up with any. While many people are petrified of public speaking, she was happy to talk to her great granddaughter's class for over an hour. Cards, cruises, parties, balls—bring it on. She likes all kinds of music, likes fashion, and loves parties and people. In short, she has a love affair with life."

–Anti-Aging Psychologist Dr. Michael Brickey
Michael Brickey, Ph.D., ABPP
America's Anti-Aging Psychologist
Ageless Lifestyles Institute, LLC
865 College Ave.
Columbus, OH 43209 USA
614-237-4556
DrBrickey@DrBrickey.com
www.DrBrickey.com
http://www.Anti-Aging-Speaker.com
Author's Note: Dr. Brickey's book <u>Defy Aging</u> was a Finalist in *Foreword* magazine's "Book of the Year Awards" and his book <u>52 Baby</u>

<u>Steps to Grow Young</u> was a Finalist in the "Fresh Voices" and in the "Best Books" awards.

Elsa became fast friends with award winning author, Lynn Peters Adler, J.D., Founder of the National Centenarian Awareness Project. Lynn presented a Centenarian Certificate to Elsa on her 100th birthday. Mrs. Peters Adler was also instrumental in expanding Elsa's celebrity nationally through setting up Elsa's interview with  Barbara Walters. Her goals overlap mine: to recognize and respect the wisdom of our elders, as well as to promote positive aging and living with inspiring examples like Elsa. Her book is called <u>Centenarians: The Bonus Years</u>.

"An inspiration and role model for living long and living well, Elsa's life has been successful, fulfilling and happy, with her golden years '*like sparkling diamonds!*' Her positive attitude plays a major role. On the go, beautifully dressed, she sets an example by taking good care of herself, and her sense of humor makes for delightful company. She loves a party and enjoys making others happy; the song "Cabaret" comes to mind -- I want to be like Elsa!"

Lynn Peters Adler, J.D.
Founder and Director, National Centenarian Awareness Project
Lynn Peters Adler, J.D.
National Centenarian Awareness Project
website: adlercentenarians.org
email: adler@ncap100s.org
office: 800.243.1889

Douglas Buce interviewed Elsa in 2008

"Grace, dignity, wisdom, wit, and charm naturally flow from this magnificent lady. Her stories are inspiring, and her spirit is contagious. After meeting with Elsa Hoffmann in her home where I was so graciously welcomed, I learned valuable lessons about life, business, and relationships. One thing was crystal clear in my mind as I was saying goodbye to her that day... I want to be just like Elsa."

Doug Buce
President, Wells University
Wells Real Estate Funds
Norcross, GA
wellsref.com

Pat Russel Anderson is an internationally recognized artist for her nautical and tropical artwork, as well as an active community member and author. She owns a store in Lighthouse Point, FL called *My Own Cruising Journal.* She and her parents were friends and visitors to the Jasmin Villa Resort when Elsa and Bill owned it. These are some of her memories that she also included in a beautiful 2009 calendar she created celebrating art from coastal living and boat parades. It also includes history and paintings she did illustrating her wonderful cruising experiences with her late husband "Capt. Pete."

Photos included in Pat Anderson's "My Own Cruising Journal" and calendar were taken when the Russel's stayed at the Hoffmann's Motel Resort: Jasmin Villa in Pompano Beach, 1950's

"Backyard grilling 1950's. Shuffleboard. Tourists having fun.

Christmas Holidays with the Hoffmann family at their Jasmin Villa resort motel were special parties to entertain the tourists who would vacation there for a week, or a month. Traditional foods, tinsel on the Christmas tree, greeting cards decorated hallways, music and singing were tourist/family times to celebrate the season and enjoy the Florida sun, shuffleboard games, poolside barbecues, Florida 50's lounge chairs, the ocean swimming, white sand, vast beach of Pompano Beach. It was a time of developing as a tourist spot. The Hoffmann's were pioneers of coastal living!

Pam (Elsa's youngest child) and I were the youngest amidst those tall grownups. Duke (Elsa's youngest son, also called Gail) home from the Army, got money in a sock ornament hung on the tree. Elsa & Bill always great hosts making wonderful memories for their guests, many became lifelong friends. Today, the Hoffmann ladies and Duke shop in my retail clothing store right here in Pompano Beach.

I remember Elsa had always lots of time for everyone...even me and the tourist kids at the motel. She still takes the time to send a card, shared time with me and my husband Pete Anderson and still entertains with vigor. Pete and I celebrated her 95th Birthday Gala at the Deerfield Beach Golf & Country Club and 100th Birthday Gala at Brooks Restaurant, both local to the Pompano Beach area.

Since I have been active with the Greater Pompano Beach Chamber of Commerce as a Director and planner of the Boat Parades...we invited

Elsa to be our Grand Dame and this event will be spectacular on Sunday evening Dec. 14th 2008 on the Intracoastal Waterway. The parade will be passing the prior location of the Jasmin Villa with hundreds of homes and buildings lining the waterway."

Pat Russel Anderson
Pompano Holiday Boat Parade Artist every year since 2002
Artist, Author, Friend
website: mocj.com

As shown in the photo, Pat was commissioned to do the artwork for The Seminole Hard Rock Winterfest Boat Parade in 2007. She gave Elsa this painting on Elsa's 100th birthday. It is called the "Seminole Wave."

Internationally acclaimed artist Pat Russel Anderson presenting painting to Elsa for her 100th birthday

Introduction

<u>Blue Zones</u>: areas known for human longevity, predominantly found outside of the United States; Blue represents the "Blue Hairs" as young Floridians call the seniors there; but most importantly, Blue also symbolizes wisdom, spirituality, intelligence, healing, power, integrity, sincerity, knowledge, truth and faith.

Elsa's Own Blue Zone

America's Centenarian Sweetheart's Insights for Positive Aging and Living

With a Focus on Baby Boomers and Beyond

As a "Baby Boomer", I can relate to many of the challenges my fellow Boomers face. We want things now and we'll work hard for them. Nevertheless, all that working has left us drained, undersexed, overmedicated and out-of-balance. As we seek out current and past great luminaries to figure this all out for us, we often ignore the real people right in front of us that also can help guide us through many of our struggles: seniors that are our relatives, friends, co-workers and neighbors (seriously). It's a well known fact that many other

1

cultures around the world have a deep reverence and respect for their elders. Their life experience is important to seek out for help with life's decisions and challenges. America, unfortunately, has more of a reputation closer to what the ancient Alaskans did according to Alaskan writer Velma Wallis' "fables"... abandoning their oldest tribe members in the snowy wilderness to die if they became a burden to the Alaskan nomads.

Luckily for me, I have a remarkable person in my life who has been hugely instrumental as an inspiring role model to me and to countless others, and who now has become a celebrity centenarian figure representative of positive living and positive aging in a way people find to be unbelievable. Part of our learning curve here is to release our visuals of what we think "old age" is, and to embrace what the new possibilities are. My grandmother, Elsa Brehm Hoffmann, was born October 11, 1907. No one who meets her can fathom that this attractive woman with a young demeanor is anywhere near 100. People are always asking what her "secrets" are. When she appeared on Barbara Walter's primetime special on April 1, 2008, entitled "How to Live to 150 – Can You Do It?" Elsa told Barbara her golden years are like "sparkling diamonds." She also shared photos of the birthday present she got herself for her 100th birthday, a new car! She has more physical and mental agility than many seniors years younger. The insights in this book will help you understand how Elsa has cultivated and continues to maintain her fulfilling life, and how you can do it, too.

Since genes are only 25% of longevity, there are other things at work. Sure, there's a strong faith, social interaction, some basic weight control, sun protection and moisturizer happening, but the little things she does and the thought processes she uses are the true magic that has produced a beautiful life spanning over 100 years. And for those skeptics that think only the very wealthy can live this positive happy long life --- Rest assured you do not need to be wealthy or famous to make greater leaps towards happiness with the simple steps enclosed.

While contemplating the writing of this book, I sought out feedback as to what is helpful information to share of my vast array of observations, family stories, and philosophies that Elsa represents. While books similar to the subject may have shared stories of inspiration,

2

people thought these publications would give them some simple day to day basics that they could easily incorporate into their own lives, but this was not the purpose or the result of those books. Other studies reflect how longevity is achieved in vastly different and more primitive lands than our industrialized America. Those resources confirm how healthy habits are indeed important. Nevertheless, Elsa demonstrates an exhilarating and extraordinary example of how to have a happy life beyond adhering to these basics, and perhaps most revealing, within the joys and challenges of the *modern* world.

This compilation of Elsa's insights is knowledge to enhance your happiness daily. My aim is to at least begin to fill that desire Boomers and others seek for a more joyous and fulfilling life by examples they can use now and continue to build upon. I also incorporate how I use Elsa's insights in my own life as a Baby Boomer for this positive living, occasionally expounding upon that with additional strategies I have learned from my studies on pertinent luminaries of our time. And, of course, any Baby Boomer worth her salt is going to use real life humor in explaining many points, too.

We all better start changing how we feel about positive aging, in addition to positive living, because we're up next. The US Census Bureau estimated a count of about 95,000 U.S. centenarians in 2008, projected to be over one million by 2050. Scientists predict that a girl born today has a 50% chance of living to 100 or more, and one out of three fifty year old women today will live to ninety. The experts on the Barbara Walters longevity show said a baby born today could live to 150. AOL's Health News (Prevention) reported in November 2008 that the average life expectancy increased by 30 years in the 20th century (within the United States); the greatest gain in 5,000 years. The number of centenarians increased 51% from 1990 to 2000. This news also cited how seemingly unimportant everyday habits can influence how long and how well you live, such as eating purple foods like berries. Elsa's simple steps that have enhanced her life will detail many more easy great habits and philosophies that help her, and can help you.

Rather than permeating old age stereotypes either consciously or subconsciously, we need to very consciously start portraying a positive and radiant attitude on aging to our children (and to ourselves) as each generation lives longer. There's no turning back, so let's make every year as fulfilling as it can be. Each generation makes great contributions to the world, however by listening to the wisdom of our elders, we can do it all while enjoying life more.

So what is preventing us from more positive living and aging? We are often consumed with planning ahead and worrying. We have grasped that we should be living in the moment, however doing that often eludes us. We are so overly busy. We get so used to our company SOP's (standard operating procedures) that give us the step-by-excruciating-step of how to complete a task. Without that guideline, we risk feeling lost. This training may be necessary for business, but unfortunately spills over into our regular lives to an extent that we cannot tap into our own inner wisdom to live in a continual fulfilling state. We have an internal compass to help us in our lives for living well, however we are too stressed out and overbooked to just not feel guilty about taking time to relax listening to this inner wisdom.

To get back to this natural fulfilling state, we have to not just read about this being a truth, but take mini easily doable steps to get back to that healthy balance and to tune into it. We need SOPs for living to get us on track again. Elsa's life examples teach you her invaluable insights.

Some things I have learned from Elsa seem so simple, although when actually practiced, they are quite effective for positive living experiences. Regardless, even with her being someone I want to emulate, I sometimes give in to the other very strong pressures in our culture and later regret doing so. For example, whenever I get the list of specialty summer camps or after school activities to let our children try, my first instinct is to sign them up for practically everything! Our Boomer generation does not want to miss opportunities for ourselves or for our children, even when it takes us beyond our budgets and time constraints. For ourselves, how many times do we join a gym, only to go for less than the contract length? It's not just about time management. It's about controlling outside pressures and ego in exchange for listening within in order to live a happier more balanced existence.

This may sound like tough love common sense in some regards. However, I truly believe Elsa's life philosophies will bring home to you how to once and for all incorporate more happiness into your life. This is done with real life examples and inspiration you can remember and use. Many of the stories may stay with you much longer, if not indefinitely, compared to, or in addition to, other projects with textbook lists of do's and do-not's for better living. In many ways, it is learning through feeling and visualizing the stories related to the insights shared.

Nevertheless, the insights also include important steps to finding our way back to positive living. These examples are very manageable and easy changes to make in our lives. This is shown by sharing how Elsa has succeeded with these insights and how her philosophies have guided and helped me. Elsa's examples may be the exact course for you to take. Perhaps they may awaken within you things you have thought about because of your own inner wisdom, but up until now have ignored due to other outside forces in your life rushing you to keep up with the Joneses'. Maybe you will see you have just been letting life happen to you instead of creating your own version of heaven on earth. When we use the best demonstrated practices of real life people such as Elsa, we find a way to live positively and more joyously. Taking charge to live positively will bring better things to us and let us enjoy the here and now in the meantime. Referring to these things as a reference will keep us in the zone for good things in our lives. At the same time, we will be uplifting those around us.

Real Life Choices for More Fulfilling Living

Looking Sharp

We must never confuse elegance with snobbery.
Yves Saint Laurent

While preparing for a job interview with a perfume company right after college, I found in my research that their perfume was a consistent great seller, even during hard economic times. I found this so interesting that this item, which most would think of as an extravagance easily given up when times are tough, was not affected as one would expect.

It was a small piece of happiness women held onto to make them feel good when they started their day.

Elsa feels strongly that looking (and smelling) nice for yourself and for those you encounter during the day not only brightens your outlook, but is a sign of respect for yourself and others. Elsa's neighbor and friend, Betty Brown, describes Elsa as "always looking like she just came off the pages of *Vogue*." Even when Elsa is at home, you will not find her in an old housecoat or ripped sweats. She will be ready to go out, or will be found in one of her graceful full length peignoir sets reading, organizing, cooking, on the phone, or watching a good movie.

One day a friend who lives on her floor told me he saw what he thought was an angel in a flowing gown passing by in the middle of the night. He concluded it was Elsa, only because she was carrying laundry (They have a shared laundry room down the hall). When Elsa can't sleep, she uses the time to do laundry or polish silver (Do any Boomers still bother with or appreciate real silverware?). Anyway, you never know who might see you and when. Family members delight in telling this story again and again.

"How you look" examples come to mind for me from when my husband Mike and I spent one of our wedding anniversaries at a big, beautiful country club. Our dear cousin Nancy worked there at the time and found us a special weekend deal. The room was breathtaking, and we knew the restaurants were top notch.

Dinner was exquisite, but when the intricate and artful brunch buffet was opened the next day, we were a tad shocked to see some people showing up at this outstanding ballroom-style chandeliered restaurant in swimsuits and barely there cover-ups. Even the good bodies were so out of place. Nobody wants your tanned flaking epidermis in their cream cheese, no matter what size you are. Yuck. At least a sundress or shorts outfit would have been more "respectful" and sanitary to the other diners ... and to themselves and the restaurant. We did see, however, one employee there give a jacket to an underdressed male at dinnertime. It took finesse to do it quickly and without a fuss, but the restaurant had to draw the line somewhere in order to maintain a proper dress code and a certain ambiance within a place that people paid dearly for (even us with our deep discount).

We follow the rule that when you're not sure how dressy a place is, call ahead or just plan to dress up to be sure. I know our culture has become more and more casual; however, the memorable and fancy family dinners Elsa has planned at her home or at a restaurant all her life just wouldn't seem right if we weren't dressed up for the occasion (unless it's an outdoor pool barbecue). So, even my husband, who wasn't this way before, learned to accept this way of celebrating and respecting himself, me as his date, and the host, whether it be a restaurant or individual.

Looking nice doesn't require a lot of time, energy or expense. Elsa will just as easily buy a piece of clothing or accessory she likes at Target (aka "Tar-shea") as a fancy boutique or an upscale store like Neiman Marcus (jokingly referred to as "Needless Mark-up"; I know someone who got some fabulous leopard pattern boots there for a song!), and she always looks great.

Sprucing up your look may mean a more flattering or more modern hairstyle. Perhaps it means getting sized for the proper bra fit (come on, I've had it done; it's not as bad as getting a tooth pulled, and it can make a huge difference). And men, your bodies change, too. Don't keep trying to wear the same sized Levi's you wore in your twenties if they are too tight. All of these things I notice due to Elsa's "looking sharp" example.

If you ever watch shows such as TLC's "What Not to Wear", you can easily see the inspiring transformation when a person learns how to wear appealing and properly sized clothes for his or her own body type. So, to reiterate, dressing attractively does more for you than demonstrate respect for yourself and others: as Elsa sees it, "It also gives you a psychological lift."

You would think that looking nice consistently would be something others would see as a positive. You don't think twice about dressing nicely to go out with a friend, or to a wedding, or to religious services, so why not everywhere? I understand the "come as you are" approach when being there is the most important thing, but if you have the brief time it takes to put yourself together nicely first, why not show that respect?

This makes sense to most. Regardless, someone actually told a relative of ours that she thought Elsa had a big ego because she always looked nice. What?! I was so shocked someone thought that way that some spit came out of my mouth when I heard that. It reminds me It reminds me of the criticism some people gave Joel Osteen; they said the popular preacher smiles too much. Who are these critics, the devil's spawn? Nevertheless, you need to do things that brighten your outlook as Elsa does, and disregard the bad eggs that just don't get it. As my late dad, Richard Textor, used to remind people, "Consider the source."

Be of Good Cheer & Think Beautiful Thoughts

A man should hear a little music, read a little poetry, and see a fine picture every day of his life, in order that worldly cares may not obliterate the sense of the beautiful which God has implanted in the human soul.
Johann Wolfgang von Goethe, German writer, 1749-1832

Everyone needs beauty as well as bread, places to play in and pray in, where nature may heal and cheer and give strength to body and soul alike.
John Muir, Scottish American naturalist and conservationist, 1838-1914

Don't cry because it's over. Smile because it happened.
Dr. Seuss

No one can circumvent all negative influences from people and from life's challenges in general, but all can use some tricks to protect against them and to more quickly recover from them. Elsa has over 100 years of "beautiful things" she has seen and felt in her inventory of memories that keep her up when she feels less than positive. She just thinks about these wonderful times in her life that have brought her so much joy, and before she knows it, she is over whatever thought or situation was consuming her. To try this, you may want to write down ten things that are memories that make you laugh or make you smile that you can pull out in a jiffy as needed to alter your feelings from potentially toxic to vibrantly uplifting.

For example, my own ten things written down have included these types of memories and thoughts over the years:

* my wedding day, the adoptions of our girls, and several special holiday memories with loved ones.

* a surprise party I gave to a South American friend. As we came down the steps of the house to the party room, he was so startled to see a bunch of friends there yelling "Surprise!" that he spread out his arms and yelled "Surprise!", too, in a stunned and automatic pilot reaction.

* the feeling I had of buying my first really cool car, an Eagle Talon in polo green.

* When I initially met my husband at a club through friends, he insisted on walking me home. He said he was concerned for my safety in our rural area. He claimed there were recent "bear sightings" near my condo building.

* I gave my husband a huge surprise party for his 50th birthday. He later thanked me for a great party, but pleaded with me never to do it again because he thought it would give him a heart attack at an older age - (I guess I'm pretty good at surprising people)

* My cousin Craig recently told me that he and his family love the local organic food store, however he has given it a new name, "Whole Paycheck."

* a reminder to myself to look online for any of my favorite artists singing one of my favorite songs when I need a quick lift, or, for a disturbing, yet amusing blast from the past: the fake and famous dancing baby video

* When my mom and Elsa stayed over at our place, they were up early with our 4 and 6 year old girls. They asked the girls if they were allowed to eat candy as the children were doing so early in the morning. The girls explained, "We are allowed to eat candy early as long as Mommy and Daddy are still sleeping."

Other choices that may work for you that I have used include simply listening to music, taking a walk, calling a friend, or even reorganizing just one thing in your home or office like a file or a drawer. Just forcing yourself to smile is proven to help your attitude. Another helpful new habit is to review in your mind before you go to sleep at least five things you are grateful for that day. Say to yourself upon rising that today is going to be a fabulous day and think about the results of what you want and thank God that your desires are in the process of being received. Don't get bogged down in the details of how it will happen. Start knowing good things are on the way. Also, don't keep watching and listening to the same bad news you've already heard on the television or radio. Turn on something else or go do something else. Feed your head with some positive thoughts.

When entering into a potentially negative situation, a prayer and envisioning being encircled with protective white light works, too. Don't knock it until you've tried it! Deepak Chopra and Wayne Dyer advocate meditation for getting through challenges (Deepak has said it can be helpful even if only closing your eyes and clearing your mind from stressful bothersome thoughts for 3 minutes; Wayne has a meditation using the Lord's Prayer to clear your mind). Abraham-Hicks writings focus entirely on positive good-feeling thought and emotion guiding you through rough patches by utilizing solely The Law of Attraction (They say holding a positive thought for as little as 17 seconds makes a great impact). I recall one of my favorite lines from The X-Files, "Use whatever tools you need" in response to when one character questioned herself when she found herself frantically searching tarot cards or something similar to gain "The truth."

These ideas may seem pretty far out to my grandmother, or even to some Boomers, but I see it all as similar tools in different packaging for different people. After all, ancient cultures worshipped the sun. That made sense since that made their crops grow ... their own version of envisioning God. It all leads to the same positive feelings that create a magical happy lifetime because you can connect through these tools to your inner guide, inner wisdom, love, life force, God, or whatever you want to name it (but if it's good, it's God!). It's better to find this through non-traditional means than to end up as a toxic unhappy blob of negativism.

Moreover, some additional results of the "Elsa" way reveal more happy outcomes that spread and come back to her to keep her in such good spirits. For example, whenever Elsa sees someone she knows, or is interacting with a cashier or anyone else, she gives them all a big smile and all the same respect and courtesies. This small effort brings about more pleasant exchanges with others and special courtesies back to you.

At her grand 100th birthday party given to her by her children, well-known south Florida philanthropists as well as her excellent seamstress and professional plumber dear friends were invited and attended. You don't know what terrific friendships you may be missing out on that give you good cheer if you aren't allowing them in for whatever reason, from letting yourself feel intimidated to an over-inflated ego which has held you back from meaningful friendships. By treating everyone as a child of God (We are all "Holy Children of God" as described by author Marianne Williamson as she teaches Dr. Helen Schucman's illuminating, yet controversial <u>A Course In Miracles</u>) as fairly as possible, and realizing we are all neither below or above others and all have our unique and equally important goals within the big picture, you will feel a new comfort being who you are wherever you are..

Elsa's positive outlook seems to be a magnet to others. When I am out with her at family dinners, whether it's a casual place or a fancier place, often people from another table will stop by and introduce themselves. They say we must be celebrating something special because we all look so nice (see prior topic!) and we all are having such a great time. They specifically go right up to Elsa when this happens. It's as if she has an aura of positive vibes that attract people to her because they want to feel it too. Try some of the simple tips offered and you'll see a difference in your life, too.

Enthusiasm for Activity and Ambiance

Let the beauty we love be what we do.
Rumi, 1207-1273, Persian poet, theologian, Islamic jurist

We live in a wonderful world that is full of beauty, charm and adventure. There is no end to the adventures that we can have if we only seek them with our eyes open.
Jawaharlal Nehru, 1889-1964, major player in India's independence and politics

One of Elsa's dear friends, her cards playing partner Lucy Bergman, describes Elsa as "always planning and always seeing the glass as half full." She continues, "I've met a lot of interesting people in my life, yet I've never met anyone like Elsa." This is a great compliment, especially since Lucy once owned the famous Bush's Restaurant in Florida where she met and knew many celebrities and politicians that frequented there.

I see Elsa as always having a passion for something… always looking forward to "what's next" as the agenda always evolved on the once popular "West Wing" TV show … never a dull moment. She lives independently and is out and about usually every day. Every week Elsa has her scheduled card games with cocktails and luncheon or dinner, social and/or charitable functions that vary each week, church, shopping, and errands.

Elsa's doctor has checked her out thoroughly. He orders thorough blood tests for his patients of all ages. For Elsa's, the results all come out right down the normal range. All of her other vital signs are healthy, too. He supports her active lifestyle as long as she doesn't overdo it. This is good advice for all of us; listen to your body and rest when it tells you to … say "no" when necessary, too.

Her active lifestyle includes making things nicer for others and for herself wherever she can. For example, at the condo buildings where she lives, there were crests with the building name on them that got destroyed by Hurricane Wilma. She contacted the board to get permission to take on the project of how to replace them. She has since found the original artisan who made the crest (by coincidence because there were no records at the office of where to go) and has everything ready to go as soon as the budget is approved for the project.

In 2007 at Christmastime, Elsa was given a very attractive holiday wreath that was too big for her door, so she offered it to the building for the lobby entrance. She had to offer it several times. Unfortunately holiday decorating has become such a religious debate at condo buildings and town halls that it seems to hold up even a generous and thoughtful offer as this. With her persistence, however, the wreath was finally put up and enjoyed by residents and their guests.

At another time, when her church took down the artificial palm trees at the front of the sanctuary to clean, the area looked bare. When she asked when they would be returned, she was told they got ruined when cleaned. Elsa then gave money towards a fund to replace the beautiful and lifelike trees.

The importance Elsa places on creating and enjoying beauty reminds me of one thing Lady Bird Johnson was famous for: feeling adamant that cleaning up cities and beautifying highways "enhanced harmony and relieved tensions." Elsa makes her own environment as well as those shared with others as lovely as is within her power. When Hurricane Wilma destroyed her glass patio doors, the doors were on backorder to replace. Elsa had the temporary plywood covering the opening painted to look nicer in the meantime. That small and inexpensive idea made the living room pleasant and usable as she waited months for the new doors. Our environment is such an important part of our happiness that often is last on the to-do list. Nevertheless, perhaps Elsa's examples will help us think of our own easy solutions to enhance our environments, too.

When I assisted in Kindergarten Halloween fun with my daughter Blair's class, I had a "spooky" game to play with the children. As I saw the other mothers set up their stations, there was one for making masks, another for decorating cookies, and another for making necklaces. It was obvious that one mom had put more thought into it than the rest of us. She had a Halloween tablecloth and "scary" centerpieces that really set the mood. I thought to myself how I could have easily done that, too, if I had just made a quick trip to one of those "Dollar Stores." It looked really good and excited the kids, so of course I complimented her on the presentation. I made up for it at my table by being as enthusiastic as I could and the children did have fun. I also had some "goodie bags" they loved. Regardless, I learned some tips for next time. Whether it's for kids or grown-ups, a few extra minutes of preparation makes a noticeable difference. And, yes, I had fun, too.

As for my home, I try to have the main rooms of the house in decent shape even when there is so much else on my list. If I'm tired, I put away laundry while watching a favorite TV program and don't even realize I'm getting a lot done. If I need a nap on the weekend before starting an organizing project, I'll do it and commit to the project afterwards. When we moved to a house from our condo, we knew caring for landscaping would not be possible with our full schedule, so we bought a place in a community that does it for us for a nominal monthly fee.

Choosing where to live takes a lot of thought. In our case, it of course involved the practical things like schools, our financial limits, and taxes. Nevertheless, we did not undervalue the importance of ambiance. After living near the ocean, we didn't want to move to some townhouse overlooking a parking lot. We found a home with a gorgeous pond view. It was all that we had envisioned and more. Due to the importance we put on location, we know this home will either pay off well as an investment or will be a place for us to enjoy indefinitely.

Elsa was at our new house when we moved in during 2007. I looked forward to her assistance with furniture placement and décor. Her homes have all been so elegant and her design talents have been requested for everything from friends' table centerpieces to party decorations and fashion opinions. Elsa knows I welcome her ideas and she is free to move anything she thinks would look better another way in our home. In fact, when she was last visiting, we heard something being moved upstairs. Instead of assuming it was our children wrestling, my husband said, "I guess Elsa decided to move that club chair."

As I observed at Elsa's condo with a beautiful view, it can be relaxing just to look out at nature's beauty if you can't go one better and take a walk in it. It gives a little of that vacation escape feel if you let the feeling come to you to relieve stress. Even if you have no attractive view from home, perhaps you don't need to go far to find and take in a beautiful scene.

Simple suggestions I've learned from Elsa are just adding some fresh flowers or a bowl of fresh fruit to your home. It gives you a good feeling. Even letting the sun in or some fresh air is simple and makes a positive impact on your day. Seems too easy? You won't know until you do it.

Charitable - It's Not What You Think

We can do no great things, only small things with great love.
Mother Teresa

Charity sees the need, not the cause.
German Proverb

In about the same degree as you are helpful, you will be happy.
Karl Reiland

*I've seen and met angels wearing the disguise of ordinary
people living ordinary lives.*
Tracy Chapman

Go the extra mile. It's never crowded.
Author Unknown

I Know. You think I am going to tell you to give your 10% as described
in the Bible's Old Testament. I don't know those kinds of financial
details about Elsa, but it is important to give what you can, financially
or otherwise. Even when it's not money, you have something to give.
I also know when our family gets going to church regularly and gives
what we feel we can afford (even if less than 10%), I do notice times of
better financial comfort coming into our lives. I also know churches are
clamoring for more members and more money and I have no solution
(except a prayer) to offer for either as we all balance our time, budgets
and spiritual needs.

Back to Elsa … She does attend a wonderful church, The First
Presbyterian Church of Pompano Beach, FL (see it on pinkpres.org),
and she does give regularly. Nevertheless, when I think of "charitable"
in regards to her, I mostly think of things she does for people. If
someone in her condo building has had a loss in their family and she is
at least an acquaintance of the person, she will not only call, visit and
send a meaningful sympathy card, but I've seen her leave them cold
cuts and treats so they are prepared for family visiting. Then they do
not have to do an immediate food errand in their grief. Often in her
condo building people are far from loved ones in other states, so this
sincere care is often very needed and appreciated when loved ones have
not arrived yet. When the one mourning is a friend, she also keeps

in touch to try to bring them up and out again after everyone else has moved on (most need the comfort from loved ones, religious leaders, and/or grief support groups as well as time to heal from loss; many wonderful books help, too; books by authors George Anderson and James Van Praagh helped me through losses). Unfortunately, these acts of kindness are just not as customary as they used to be. Elsa knows the importance of these gestures, however, and this reveals her genuine love and concern for others. She does not let the pull of a busy life take her away from the simple things that are truly the most meaningful.

When Elsa has won large items at charity raffle events, she has given them away. One was a huge gourmet basket of food. She brought that over to the local municipal building that houses the police department for all to share. She had heard from my daughter Blair that her school needed a TV, so she took the large TV she won over to give to the church school Blair attended. Who thinks of that? Most would keep that gourmet basket and finish a few things only to let the rest rot and get discarded. Someone else would force that big TV into a too-small room just to keep it even though it had no comfortable place for it there (or let relatives fight over it).

When Elsa had a wound that wasn't healing, her course of treatment included being in a hyperbaric chamber (that's right, for you Michael Jackson fans, the same as he uses! We called her the Energizer Bunny because the treatment gave her even more energy than her usual!). There were other seniors there who were frightened of this treatment and the nurses asked Elsa to talk to them. She gladly obliged and was able to comfort them. Elsa also noticed that the movies there for patients to watch were all of the shoot 'em up variety, so she donated musicals such as "The Sound of Music" so patients could heal with a better and more comfortable group of thoughts (She's seeming very "Abraham-Hicks" here, huh?).

These are things we all can easily do (in addition to what $ we do give regularly) if we open ourselves up to these opportunities of giving in ways that involve little or no money, and only some of our time if we pay attention to the needs around us where we happen to be anyway. In addition, if you do have extra money or time, there's a place for that to help, too. Giving time or money transforms your heart and makes you feel terrific at the same time. Start small (or big!) and check it out.

For hard facts on the plus side of giving, there was an intriguing study done by researchers under the umbrella of The National Institute of Health. A game was played by participants while dopamine levels were monitored in the brain. Dopamine levels are said to indicate pleasure. In the game, subjects lost and gained money. They also had the opportunity to give some money to a good cause. Dopamine was highest not when money was made in the game, but when a portion of money was given away (discovered by neuroscientists Jordan Grafman and Jorge Moll).

Elsa belongs to a few groups that do charitable work. One even asked her if she would allow them to raffle her off as "A Dinner Date with the Centenarian Celebrity Extraordinaire." She said "yes." My conservative, caring, Catholic-schooled husband had a fit saying "You can't raffle off Elsa to some stranger!" As it turns out, after the bidding ended, a friend from one of her women's groups won. Elsa earned the charity $300 with that involvement.

Fads are Fun

If you obey all the rules, you miss all the fun.
Katharine Hepburn

About twenty years ago I met a friend of a friend who said she was from Persia (aka the old country name used to try and avert Americans from asking questions about Iran; It hasn't been Persia since 1935). I remember her because she was adamant about what was proper jewelry. She said "If it's not real, it shouldn't even touch your skin." At the time I was glad I had on my real pearls (one of the few "real" pieces of jewelry I owned) and I said nothing, but now, wiser and stronger from my mature adult "Elsa basic training", I would have a different reaction.

Elsa often wears some pretty nice "real" things, however her opinion is that a splash of a fad item or a good piece of costume jewelry can be a lot of fun and very attractive. To limit oneself to egotistical or ridiculous rules such as the Persian girl's above only thwarts the variety and personality you can play around with. And by the way, that "white only between Memorial Day and Labor Day" is a "rule" you can throw out, too (as long as you're not wearing your white tankini top in January to dinner) … and a little off topic, but <u>do</u> remember the rule about when to eat oysters and when not to. I was hospitalized with seafood poisoning for days with a roommate who was preparing for a colonoscopy (yes, awful all around). As the late Gilda Radner's SNL character Rosannadanna used to say, "I thought I was gonna die!"

Elsa doesn't hesitate to try something new. "You just don't know until you try it on." Often she ends up with something amazing and fresh that looks just perfect for her and gains a plethora of compliments. I have found the same. Sometimes I try something that looks kind of funky on the hanger only to find it's fabulous on.

Elsa also has purchased fabric on her travels and then had her seamstress put together something Elsa designed (I never had a seamstress except for when I lost weight once and had all my business suit skirts taken in two sizes - one of the happiest moments of my life! … and having a seamstress to fit your nice clothes properly isn't as expensive as you'd think). Again, most times this works out for a unique and attractive outfit, but on one occasion, Elsa's orange silk pants suit she had made from her own fabric, turned out like, well, an orange silk pants suit. She hated it. We all hated it. Several years later, this expensive combo of fabric and seamstress work was recycled into the best scarecrow outfit you ever saw. She won a first place at her club's Halloween party in 2006.

RSVP Promptly, Acknowledge, Thank

"Répondez s'il vous plaît"

A French phrase that translates to "please respond" and word for word translation is "respond if you please", whether you are attending or not. Judith Martin, the author of etiquette books and a syndicated newspaper columnist known as "Miss Manners," thinks that "R.S.V.P." came about as a polite way of reminding people of something that they should already know: If you receive an invitation, you should reply.

Manners are a sensitive awareness of the feelings of others. If you have that awareness, you have good manners, no matter which fork you use.
Emily Post

RCSU

Abbreviation for "Rude, crude, and socially unacceptable"
An American phrase that denotes offensive, unattractive behavior.

Rudeness is the weak man's imitation of strength.
Eric Hoffer, 1898-1983, American social writer and philosopher

Who finds a faithful friend, finds a treasure.
Jewish Saying

If you have ever planned a special party, or even a wedding, isn't it kind of disheartening when someone responds at the last minute, or not at all? What if you haven't seen them in a long while, and anticipate they will be as glad to see you as you are them, and then you receive their response via return card, email or call, with just a plain regrets? I even heard a younger Gen X guest who said on Elsa's 95th birthday that the Gen X generation doesn't RSVP. Come again? What's up with that? I guess they have only been going to frat-type parties and haven't gone through the preparation of having their own decent party where knowing how many are coming is vital to all the work, cost and energy going into the affair, whether it be a simple or fancy get-together (I am happy to report this young person seems to have totally transformed into a mature caring person within the five years since then). A prompt RSVP is necessary whether it's a child's birthday party or a grand affair.

Late responses make your mind wander. Were they waiting for a better offer, or am I so unimportant to them that they forgot about it entirely? Of course it may be none of the above, but try not to ever be in that category of late responses. Even if you think you may need to be at someone's graduation/surgery/birth/court date about that time but the exact date isn't known yet, call early to explain that you want to go, but is it possible for you to respond later after you get the date of the other thing you're definitely committed to being at first, and respond with your firm answer by such and such a date? I learned by Elsa's example that it's the least you can do to be a good friend. Show some enthusiasm, too! As Elsa's friend Joanne Swensen paraphrases Ralph Waldo Emerson, "You must be a friend to have a friend." That's why Elsa has so many friends.

Elsa always responds as promptly as possible, including a little note or call about how she looks forward to it, or with a call why she cannot attend but would have liked to. You know, there's no RSVP Police that say your message has to fit on the tiny line where you put your name. Also, if it's unclear whether you are invited with a date, or your children, or your dog - make sure to inquire with a call to be sure (but if your name is the only one on it, likely it's a one person invite). I have seen exceptions, though. One family sent an invite to the parents, but meant for it to include their grown children and thought the "yes" reply meant they all were coming. It's best to check when in doubt.

People do try to do the right thing, but they think differently. For our wedding (I was 38 and my husband was 48, his second marriage), there were just too many children total in our families, so we didn't invite children so we had enough room for all the adults we wanted to invite. Also, that's our prerogative to have an adult atmosphere for our special day. In addition, we had many unattached single and divorced friends that knew each other as friends, so they were invited as singles and seated together so we could maximize sharing our day with all our single unattached friends rather than half of our single friends with dates we didn't know. If money was no object, it may have been different, but if we had over 125 guests, we may not have had time to visit each table as well as enjoy our celebration, which we were able to do with the 125. And, of course, there are always exceptions to consider.

Ya know that feeling you have the day after you had a get-together at your place or elsewhere? You're happy you created some memories with those close to you and showed them you cared enough to have them over to relax, to celebrate, and to have fun. Isn't it nice when someone calls and says that they had a great time and thanks you for your hospitality? It doesn't have to be long or elaborate, but a note or call would be a small thing to make someone feel good. Elsa is known for her handwritten thank you notes or cheerful phone calls that evidence her sincere appreciation for being invited to a social event or an act of kindness made towards her. Thinking of making others happy makes her happy and repeats the cycle again.

Also, no matter how busy your life is or how some rules ease with the times, swiftly acknowledging the receipt of a gift is always important and polite. A call, note, or email will give the giver peace of mind that a mailed gift arrived or that you know what was given by who at a party (exception could be if the opening and thanking are done in person). Saying thanks and adding a sentence or two about what you like about it is easy to do at the same time. For monetary gifts, indicating the way you will use it or save it is a nice acknowledgement. At a minimum, even if you hate the gift, give thanks for the thoughtfulness. Your children will learn this from you prioritizing this basic foundation of being polite and showing appreciation (not to mention having class). If this is really difficult for you, there are books on the market to teach you how (see books by Rosalie Maggio or Sandra E. Lamb; others are available for business needs). It's an essential skill for personal and career emotional intelligence. This simple task enhances relationships with friends and family as well as increases good rapport with business associates.

The weekend of her big 100th birthday party, Elsa had many gifts to open despite requesting "no gifts please" on her invites. People just couldn't help themselves to get her something special. Elsa eventually opened everything, and sent out thank you notes as expeditiously as she could as she opened a group of gifts daily for a while. Before she opened anything, though, you know what she did? She called some of her good friends that could not make the party due to illness to check in on them. Who thinks of that? Elsa does. And we all should, too.

Plan Six or More Special Things Every Year

Sometimes it's important to work for that pot of gold. But other times it's essential to take time off and to make sure that your most important decision in the day simply consists of choosing which color to slide down on the rainbow.
Douglas Pagels, Author

Christmas, Easter, Thanksgiving (or other religions' and cultures' celebrations - there's at least a "Big 3")... now find at least three more days to add to them that you will plan ahead a special get-together, special event or get-away. Spread them out on your calendar today.

Elsa stays on a high of having a busy social calendar weekly (and a trip or two yearly), but for those of us still working regularly and still nurturing growing children, six big things to look forward to should be manageable and enough to help keep our "happy juices" flowing. I just took this insight and reserved hotel stays for three short trips within Florida for the next three times we can take a one to three nights trip due to a holiday or slow business period. I got good pricing for planning ahead, and I feel elated looking forward to these little getaways.

Know When to Say No To the Jelly

The art of leadership is saying no, not saying yes. It is very easy to say yes.
Tony Blair

Just about every friend, acquaintance or stranger that any of our family members run into says, "Hey, you should get Elsa put on that jelly." They are referring to the practice Smucker's has had to put a centenarian on their jelly label that former clown (that's right, a real clown, including the original Ronald McDonald clown) Willard Scott brought to light upon wishing centenarians happy birthday on his TV weather report starting in 1983, and still does now occasionally since his retirement when he covers for Al Roker on The Today Show.

Smucker's has some fine and popular products, but Elsa does not want to be on the jelly. It's a nice recognition, and a lot of fun for many, but it's not her thing. No offense, Smucker's. You have left a lot of people happy and smiling with this practice, but it's not for everyone. Elsa has made herself clear on this one. She listens to her inner guidance system and it has served her well in small and in big matters. End of story.

Sometimes we hear something so much that we eventually just give into it even though that's not really what we want to do. Don't do it. Stick to your guns on a principle when collaborating or compromising really leaves no benefit (except to stop hearing the same thing from others all the time). It would just leave the result of making you feel badly that you gave in. Let the others just give up and stop trying to influence you rather than you giving in first to stop the madness.

When my husband and I decided that adopting was the way we wanted to make a family together, not all were so supportive. Some couldn't fathom how in our 40's (me) and 50's (Mike) we could balance running our business and starting a family this "late." What about the background and the health of the families of these children? How could we love them as our own? How would it affect our retirement (hah. What retirement?)? Even my mom and Elsa thought it may be a bit too much for us, especially as we considered adopting two children at the same time (although they now are overjoyed and enriched by having these children in their lives). We knew what we wanted, however, and were up to the challenges. There are no guarantees on the health and gene mix in families who have their biological children, so expecting perfection in adoptions was not expected by us, either. After a lot of research, we found that for our ages, income, home size (a condo at the time), desire to adopt two children at once as young as possible, and desire to complete all as soon as possible, Russia was the best route for adoption for us in 2004. We also found an excellent and reputable agency to work with and met families they had brought together.

When people have the audacity to question why we didn't adopt domestically (especially in that "holier-than-thou" voice), I cannot even answer properly with less than an hour to explain completely (and to me, there are things like caring for God's children that we must look at from a spiritual and a global perspective; the need is within and beyond our borders - we can make great impact here and elsewhere simultaneously. This is a belief adjustment and update for many to consider and adapt). There are many variables that make a good adoption match for a particular family.

Our research on the best country match for us started domestically, then went to China, and ultimately ended up as Russia. It is not a simple answer and each family has different circumstances to consider and offer. So, in our case, after refinancing our home and taking our two trips to Russia (and all the other details in-between including an evaluation of us and our home, extensive paperwork, medical review of us and of the girls, etc.), we were home with our two little miracles in 2004, Blair Marie, at age 3, and Elsa Anastasia, 14 months, within nine months from start to finish. It's hard to believe the many physical and personality features these girls have that blend in so well with our family. I believe these souls were really meant to be with us and we were spiritually guided to them. There is no question in my mind that there is a God given grand plan and they were part of it for us.

So know when to stick to your guns to just say no to the unwanted jelly in your life.

Calendar of Events

Don't agonize. Organize.
Florynce Kennedy, Civil and Women's Rights Activist, lawyer, 1916-2000

One must be organized to keep up with a busy schedule with friends and family. Elsa does this by keeping a mini office near her kitchen phone. She has an attractive den that has a desk and also serves as a guest room, however she has found her best space to keep her calendar organized. She is one to pay attention to the details. Elsa will be there and be on time. If appropriate, she will also bring favors or participate in a theme. Planning and decorating, from clothing to decorated hats, brings a sense of playfulness for all. In addition, it's stress-free because Elsa organizes ahead of time.

Elsa no longer has the big house in Rye, NY, the location of some grand parties in the 1960's that people still recalled at her 100th birthday party (people also long remembered get-togethers she had at a smaller place she and her husband had prior to that). She continues to entertain through the club she belongs to and at local restaurants for special occasions, including her fabulous 100th birthday party with nearly 200 guests. Her condo home is nestled in a marvelous location on the intracoastal waterway in south Florida with the ocean across the street. She has also used the attractive condo clubhouse for some memorable family get-togethers.

I thought I was pretty organized until we adopted our children. Suddenly there were so many priorities and the mail doesn't get attended to right away and laundry builds up faster than time to get it done. I still keep a "to-do" list in a small notebook and calendar in my purse, but I do not expect to get all done in the timeframes I used to. Get it done in your own realistic timeframe.

One of our family stories we enjoy about how organized Elsa has always been is about the preparations she would do when there was a big party at her house in Rye. The roofers at their business would come over to help get the party tent set up. She would hire a couple of women to help with other things, and she would even plan out how the helpers should lay out the food with a buffet diagram. On one occasion, guests were already arriving and Elsa was having a cocktail and conversing with her guests. One of these helper women ran out of the kitchen towards the group looking for Elsa, yelling, "Mrs. Hoffmann, Mrs. Hoffmann! I have lost my diaphragm!"

Root Canal Relaxation

If people concentrated on the really important things in life, there'd be a shortage of fishing poles.
Doug Larson, Author & Outdoorsman

Don't underestimate the value of Doing Nothing, of just going along, listening to all the things you can't hear, and not bothering.
Pooh's Little Instruction Book, inspired by A.A. Milne

Taking a bath is Elsa's favorite relaxation ritual. It's not just any bath. It has to be a soak with that beautifully aromatic VitaBath gel (and it has to be the green kind). In fact this is such an enjoyable way to wind down for her, that instead of just giving it up after turning 100 when she noticed getting out of the tub seemed a little more difficult than usual, she opted to start an exercise regimen to strengthen her arms and back (as recommended by her doctor). She has a professional work with her two times a week, and she also does the exercises at home herself. That decision to give such emphasis to observing a ceremony that balances, restores, relaxes, and allows for revitalizing oneself for the next project, challenge or social event, is a wise one. In our pie pieces of what's important, something representing relaxation for balance needs to be there.

For other relaxation, Elsa also likes classic movies, reading historical-based fiction, and allows herself to nap when needed. Although that sounds like a singles ad (perhaps with the exception of the "nap" part), it's just meant to give you an idea of some ways to decompress! … and something to prioritize.

I recall being so stressed with school or work or whatever when I was single and lived up north, that coming down yearly to be with Elsa was something I often craved to get recharged. I would stock up on magazines so I wasn't even committing myself to finishing a book while on my vacation. I had "*Cosmo*", of course, and one day Elsa thought reading one of my magazines might be relaxing for her, too. Well, once she saw some of the racy subject matter, she wanted no part of it. When she was young, she recalled magazines of this type were all about fashion and crafts and cooking. It was a wake-up call to me about all the years my grandmother has seen, and that everyone's idea of relaxing will be different based on many factors.

Now that we live in warm weather year round, I do not get that craving to be somewhere else far from here (guess I was never much of a cold weather or snow fan), but I do get exhausted from life's daily grind. We allow ourselves naps on the weekend no matter what the "to do" list looks like. We also take advantage of local festivals on weekends and short excursions out-of-town when we can close the business for a long holiday weekend (and when we've had some good months of selling with extra disposable income to spend). A little change of scenery can be very relaxing and soul refreshing.

And oh, regarding this section's title, one of the moms I know through church asked me how I'm adjusting to my new 1.5 hour commute (each way) to work since we moved recently. I told her I'm tired, but enjoy the "quiet time for Mommy." The mother of four said she can relate. Recently she experienced a similar tranquility by thoroughly enjoying time to herself as she got off her feet and laid back

… for a root canal. A regular plan is optimal, but sometimes we gotta take it when we can get it.

Do Not Be Intimidated

You have to learn the rules of the game. And then you have to play better than anyone else.
Albert Einstein

Don't be embarrassed by making a mistake. People may notice your error briefly, if at all. They're more concerned about themselves and how they appear to others. Step outside of yourself. Consider how small this is in the big life picture. What will it matter a year from now? Pick yourself up and move on to something positive. Move on to what's next.
Sharon Textor-Black

Confidence comes not from always being right but from not fearing to be wrong.
Peter T. McIntyre

If you hear that someone is speaking ill of you, instead of trying to defend yourself you should say: "He obviously does not know me very well, since there are so many other faults he could have mentioned."
Epictetus, Greek philosopher with the Stoics, AD 55-c.135

I was very shy as a child. My mother always said how amazing her children were, but something told me she may be a bit biased on the matter. Even through most of high school, I felt easily intimidated as much as I tried to break out of it as a cheerleader (come on cheerleader-haters, don't judge; it was a great way in the country for me to utilize my years of dance and acrobatics lessons and get some exercise), student council representative, Sunday school teacher and as a team captain for the fairly new girls' track & field in the late 70's. I even was the hometown "queen" in the late 70's after my mom's prodding to go for it.

College helped me become more confident as I amazed myself when I became president of Zeta Tau Alpha sorority at Rutgers. I was probably one of the least financially secure among them (although I didn't let on of course). I was most likely from the smallest most rural town of all these girls, too. Nevertheless, they liked me and entrusted me to represent them. Working in the corporate world helped me some, but I found the politics so distressing that after almost 20 years of that, with a few small-time jobs in-between, I found my complete confidence upon having a business with my husband. I wish it didn't take so long, but without the love and support of my husband and mother, and Elsa's confident example, I never would have gotten there at all. Living near her since 2000 has many benefits! In addition, my parents and grandparents taught me valuable lessons about emotional intelligence by their example. That knowledge helped me attain personal and career goals as I developed my confidence (although identified under different names since the early 1900's, the most recent and mainstream book on this topic is <u>Emotional Intelligence: Why it Can Matter More Than IQ</u>, by Daniel Goleman).

Elsa does not come across as having a big ego, but she does portray a quiet confidence. Our daughters feel, however, that she can do anything! Whether they break their toothbrush or get holes in their tights, they say, "MiMi can fix it!" (All of us grandchildren and great-grandchildren call her "MiMi"). I loved the time when they asked Elsa if she could sew something for them, and she said, "Sure, I'd be happy to." Then they started to say "I think I can, I think I can" like "The Little Engine That Could" story. Elsa responded, "I know I can! I know I can!" Now that's a great role model!

Once when I was staying with Elsa on my vacation, we went to a very elegant restaurant for my last evening with her. Everything was delightful, but when Elsa had a yen for some port wine, she didn't get the expected reply of "Yes, madam", or "Very Good, madam." The waiter said in a stuffy English butler type of tone, "Well, what kind? We have many types." I would have probably been flustered or embarrassed, thinking I should have known that, but Elsa in her wisdom knowing no one can know about everything, responded in such a way as to not react or offend. She simply said, "Never mind." Perhaps you had to be there to see the brilliance of it, but the waiter quickly turned into his other personality and said, "Oh, I just thought of one I believe you will really enjoy, I'll bring it to you." She enjoyed her port wine and I learned one of her important lessons at the same dinner.

Moreover, it is just not important how someone else views you if you have made an innocent or silly error, or even if you didn't but someone else thinks you did. As a child in the 60's, I remember a girl a few years older than me was swimming with a group of us at a neighbor's pool. Her bathing suit top had not been tied securely and it fell down briefly. We all were so shocked. As the boys screamed, she seemed so calm. I asked her, "Isn't that so embarrassing?" She replied, "If I act embarrassed and upset, it will only egg on the boys to keep making comments." She was right. Minutes later we were all playing again as if nothing happened.

Do not hesitate to get a mentor or read some books on the topic if you lack confidence. My life is so enhanced to understand my strength and engage in life more fully because of it. I often think of Woody Allen's quote "Eighty percent of success is showing up." Marianne Williamson inspires me with her quote used by Nelson Mandela in his 1994 inaugural speech, saying, "Our deepest fear is not that we are inadequate. Our deepest fear is that we are powerful beyond measure. It is our light, not our darkness, that frightens us most. We ask ourselves, 'Who am I to be brilliant, gorgeous, talented, and famous?' Actually, who are you not to be? You are a child of God. Your playing small does not serve the world. There is nothing enlightening about shrinking so that people won't feel insecure around you. We were born to make manifest the glory of God that is within us. It's not just in some of us; it's in all of us. And when we let our own light shine, we unconsciously give other people permission to do the same. As we are liberated from our own fear, our presence automatically liberates others."

Only in America

Elsa has had several careers and has prioritized travel as part of her plans and budget for as long as I can remember. I got her one of those framed travel maps for her 100th birthday. I had to order extra pins because she used up the first batch quickly as she recalled all her trips. Her travels have taken her around the world several times and she has thoroughly welcomed every second of every journey. She always makes it clear she loves America most. Elsa often has said, "The conveniences and opportunities here are found nowhere else in the world."

Elsa's parents, Gretchen (Ahlers) Brehm and Otto Brehm, came here from Germany in 1898 as mere sixteen year-olds. They met on the steam ship voyage to America. Ironically, Elsa's mom Gretchen was born in Bremen, Germany, the ship was called The Bremen, and she married Otto Brehm from Baden, Germany. Gretchen had a job waiting for her in Chicago. Otto worked as an apprentice in Yonkers, NY. Gretchen and Otto married in 1904. They started their own bakeries and made a family together, later founding a bakery supplies business.

Gretchen and Otto celebrated their golden wedding anniversary not only as a milestone of their fifty years married, but also to commemorate fifty years in the baking business. Their grand party in 1954 was held at the Gramatan Hotel in Bronxville, New York. There were 162 guests, including family as well as city, county and state officials. Otto was known as "The Daddy of the Retail Bakers of Westchester County." In a newspaper article about the event, Otto explained how he organized the interests in his company. The reporter noted Otto Brehm had set it up "to provide a continuity of life for the business as a reward for his children because they assisted him with the venture."

Son Ernest became the new president of the company in 1956. During his tenure as president, he received an award for "Small Businessman of the Year." He did a wonderful job continuing the growth and prosperity of the company. Ernest's son Ernie Jr. took over as president and owner in 1986. Ernie Jr. recalls he learned much from his father who was a great role model for him. He also is extremely grateful for the hard work and dedication of the over 100 employees working there. The company continues to prosper. Even though few family members are still connected to the business, Elsa greatly admires the history and endurance of this business founded by her parents.

I try to imagine what it must have been like for Gretchen and Otto adjusting to a new land and language. I learned that they were anxious and proud to become American citizens as soon as possible. Also, to my surprise, Elsa told me she did not learn German from her parents, but in

Lutheran school. Having your family's first generation of American born children learn English as their first language? Now that's a novel idea! They kept their German culture with friends, music and German-themed picnics, but her parents learned English as fast as possible. Because her parents spoke English, they were able to work well with many other hard working English-speaking legal immigrant workers in the industry, including many Jewish, Polish and Italian bakery owners. Of course they had German bakery associates that were friends, too.

As her dad and mom started their bigger bread and butter (no pun intended) bakery supplies business when their Elsa was a young girl, she was the first paid employee there and was sent to business school to help her parents build the base to this business. The company continues to prosper thanks to hard work by many, but especially to these dedicated hard-working founders of the business. Their timing and foundation planning for this made-to-last business were flawless. As the oldest living past employee, the only living child of her parents who founded the business, and her work with the foundation-building of the business, she deserves some kind of medal at the very least! All of the family remains so proud of her auspicious contribution to a business that continues to thrive, and of all the achievements she has made since that time.

My husband and I know something about risk and fear as you set up your own business venture, even on our much smaller scale than what my maternal great-grandparents took on together. To think Elsa's parents came over on a boat from Germany in the late 1800's …then learned a new language as they apprenticed in new jobs apart from each other as teens … then gained the foresight, strength, money and experience to morph it all into a beautiful family and phenomenal business undertaking …. and set it up to support generations to come … is practically mind blowing to me. It was a full family effort with Elsa's dad often working at night to prepare the business for the day. This kind of multi-year and multi-generational determination, persistence and work ethic is pure inspirational American ingenuity, passion and teamwork.

I also love America and our opportunities here, but being of German and Dutch descent, I admit I sometimes wondered what life would be like living in one of those countries compared to here. The closest I ever got to dreaming of Holland kind of fell flat when I was in my twenties and met this beautiful tall Dutch girl. She wasn't very friendly and insulted me and others saying things like "You Americans say you love everything... food, your cat, your home, your family, your car ... throwing around the word love like that is ridiculous!" I should have realized that was my real first exposure of how other countries have such strong negative opinions of Americans for reasons that really can be baffling (and maybe others not so baffling).

Years later, in 2004, my husband and I adopted our two little beautiful girls from Russia. Since I am German descent, I thought surely our long stopover in Frankfurt would give me some sort of special feeling. Well, after getting the worst allergy attack of my life from walking through the airport's indoor smoking area that seemed to spread thick smoke throughout the building despite being designated in one area, we stopped to ask a roving customer service person for directions and were assisted only after she rolled her eyes and took a deep breath (I could read her mind as well as if she had a big bubble over her head with these words in them: "All these Americans expect everyone to help them"). Then I went to the convenience store to try and find some allergy medicine. I hadn't needed any in so long due to non-smoking areas in America that I didn't have any in my purse. The pretty, yet heavily pierced, bleached and tattooed young girl behind the desk was reading on a high stool behind the counter. I tried my best in my barely remembered high school German (from 26 years earlier) to ask if they had any medicine area "Haben Sie ein allergy medicine?" Between that pitiful, yet sincere attempt at Germglish and my obvious "German descent" looks, I thought I was making headway with one of "my people." She looked at me baffled and annoyed. I then said "What about aspirin?" Her scornful reply: "YOU MUST GO TO PHARMACIA!" (What is that, anyway? Angry Spanglish? She scared me!).

In addition to this bursting of my bubble (and lack of allergy relief), there must have been at least five men during our trip that came right up to Mike speaking everything from German, to French, to Russian. He had no second language background except for Latin mass with very limited Latin classes in high school (as opposed to my four years of high school German and dutiful practice in learning Russian phrases prior to this trip). When Mike said "only English", the response was almost horrific in their disbelief. I understood one couple say in German we would soon be yelling "Helfe, helfe!" in Russia, but I wasn't ready to try another phrase in German for a while to tell them we won't be yelling "Help, help!" because we were meeting up with an interpreter! I thought it must be a cultural thing for all to just approach "the man", but even if so, when we hit ground in Moscow and met our interpreter, she soon expressed to me how "European" my Irish/German/Dutch descent husband Mike looked and that I was sooo American-looking. So much for my international appeal and ethnic descent identity…

This whole experience above reminds me of the New York Bureau Chief of the Washington Post, Keith Richburg, often seen on news programs. He makes the point a bit more eloquently and seriously about his ethnic heritage. He was The Washington Post's Bureau Chief in Africa (Nairobi) from 1991-1995. He says stuff like "Afrocentrism has been fashionable for American Blacks searching for identity, but it cannot work for me. I feel no connection to this strange and violent place. Africa chewed me up and spit me out again." Wow. I once saw him on a news show telling the story of an African American group that went back to Africa to their roots to live. They were so elated to get there that they threw their passports into the ocean. As they tried to mingle with their tribe brethren whose forefathers had originally sold their ancestors into slavery, no one seemed to care about the American Blacks or their ancestors who were sold to slavery. There was no special feeling found there for the African descent Americans themselves, either. Soon they were in the ocean diving for their passports to get back as soon as possible to the opportunities and conveniences of the United States, their true home.

I'm no major world traveler, but I took an opportunity to go to Ireland in 1994. I do recall the breathtaking landscapes, but I must admit I missed the convenience of American rest stops and Seven Elevens as I traversed the country. Other than the greener than green landscapes, I recall visiting Ireland's Aran Islands on a rainy day. I heard a fishermen's sweater vendor say to his friend as I departed from the tour van in my red hooded rain slicker with matching umbrella, "Here come the Americans in their snorkel gear."

On another occasion during the same trip, I was in a small fancy restaurant. It was the type where the tables are extremely close to each other to maximize the space. I have been to them in America cities, too. I also know studies have been done that reveal Americans need more

33

personal space than people in other cultures (I once stopped dating someone who pushed his finished dishware into my space while I was still dining; we all have our quirks ... and my girlfriends often agreed with my other "biggie": if he's got bad/ugly shoes, he's not the one, even though my mom insisted I could get their shoes changed. I dunno.).

Anyway, it was no surprise to me when the close dining proximity to strangers started to make me feel uncomfortable. The table next to us, consisting of two English businessmen, asked where my travel companion and I were from. Since I was getting used to everyone we met in Ireland calling America "The States", I responded we were from "The States." They laughed, and one said, "We *know* that. *Which* state?" Later, as dessert time approached, they were a little ahead of us eating. One asked me what I had decided on for dessert. I smiled as I replied, "I want to see what your dessert looks like first." He then said to his dinner companion, "That's typical American. They always say 'you first'." Even though other English people I've met were exceptionally nice, these two rubbed me the wrong way. Could it be because they were correct on the "you first" thing? Nahhhhh. Ironically, Mark Twain once said, "An Englishman is a person who does things because they have been done before. An American is a person who does things because they haven't been done before." So there. Touché, my friend (better late than never).

A Colombian friend explained to me when I visited his homeland with him in 1992 that one does not sit by the police at a restaurant in Colombia. I said "Why not? ... Wouldn't that be safer because of kidnappings that he had told me about?" He said "No ... if guerilla terrorists are in town, they'll come in and gun down the police officers eating as well as anyone in their wake." Then I understood more clearly why uniformed men with big machine guns were stationed all around the perimeters of the Bogota Airport, and why whoever was driving us always drove like a speeding bat out of hell when travelling in-between cities.

When driving in the city of Bogota, I was the only person in the car who questioned why the city traffic flows opposite the arrows on the road after a certain time of day. Everyone kind of smiled and nodded yes, saying, "Yeah, we guess that's kind of strange to others, but normal to us". The other odd thing that took some getting used to was the regular electricity black-outs (not good for an American girl with several plug-in hair drying and curling tools). My precious memories of Colombia included meeting the very poor boy that my friend supported through a charitable organization. The underground salt cathedral made by miners was unforgettable. Seeing the inner workings of a Colombian banana farm was very impressive, too.

Moving on to thoughts of Japan, I have a second cousin Richard Brehm who is nine years older than me. While I was in elementary school, he was an exchange student in Japan. He had met Neil Armstrong (yes, that one ... "That's one small step for man, one giant leap for mankind") at a family event previously in the United States. Neil is a relative of ours through marriage (Neil's first wife Janet is Elsa's cousin). Armstrong (once). Well, before he knew it, he was on Japanese TV and being introduced as "Neil Armstrong's favorite cousin!" I guess that could have happened anywhere, but it will continue to be a great family story for years to come. And by the way, one of the questions Barbara Walters asked Elsa for the longevity show "How to Live to 150 – Can You Do It?" was, "What is the biggest event you have witnessed in your 100 years?" Elsa responded that, to her, the most fantastic was the moon landing ... the most awful was 9/11.

We have friends that are teachers in an American school in Japan. These schools cater to the children of those working there in big American corporations, children from America and elsewhere. They informed us that due to the view on karma in Japan, if you fall down onto the subway tracks, no one will help you unless a westerner is there to do it. The Japanese feel everyone needs to face whatever bad happens to balance their karma. On the other hand, even though our friends' quarters in Japan are small without a full kitchen, our friends like being able to afford a full-time nanny there. In addition, they have been able to make real estate investments outside of Japan. They also value their family sailboat trips and being fully immersed in their strong Christian faith. One thing I have heard from them, as well as others living outside of the United States, is that shopping in Japan isn't full of the dizzying amount of choices (like with cereals) we have in America.

Although there are countries that work long days as we do in the U.S., I have been told they do it at a more reasonable and less stressful pace. They also take their time at meals and breaks. Europeans and others have plenty of vacation time (37 days off in France, 42 in Italy, and 34 days for Brazilians versus 13 days average in the U.S.). That's something to copy to increase our happiness and longevity! Imagine (but then you also have to take less convenience and less services than we are used to here … like setting up phone service, which my South American friends say can take weeks to get in many places there).

I went with my Colombian friend to his country for his brother's wedding during the trip mentioned earlier. My friend had been in America several years from college to his first job as an electrical engineer. He would tell me how it amazed him how orderly things were here, and also how many laws and rules we had.

When we were in Colombia, his experiences in America definitely influenced his comments there, too. He was upset as he saw the formal family photos being taken without him and others. There were no announcements of who should go where. The casualness of the process started to get him annoyed as he was now used to the regimentation of American weddings and events. Nevertheless, it was nothing that couldn't be cured with rushing over to get in some photos as he sipped his aquadente (firewater).

For myself, I had fun being pampered in a salon before the wedding as all the women were (false eyelashes, model make-up, manicure, hair … the works!). I never looked better! I recall how I admired that every generation enjoyed and danced to the same music. In our American melting pot, we often are separated by generation with our musical preferences, especially with dance music.

More recently I conversed with a driver who took me to a rental car while my car was being serviced. He shared his experiences of living in France several years earlier. He said that in France, if you had a cold, you could get a doctor's note to stay home and rest for a month. You still got a paycheck, and medical care was covered in full. That sounded great until he also told me the tax rate to handle all this was 21% of your pay. The French full taxes total is complicated; it has been said to be about 45% of a paycheck! (I only minored in economics, so I cannot dissect that any further.) No matter if you never got sick or often were sick, everyone contributed. Since my driver friend was used to that, he missed it. He admitted he loves living here, but he couldn't understand why his doctor here couldn't see him right away when he needed him for something of a non-serious nature. Since I understand the set-up here with making appointments, I just did not relate to his concern on immediate non-urgent appointments (especially if I had to pay so dearly for the option as he did in France).

The same kind of exchange occurred in my mind when I listened to a series on National Public Radio. It was about government regulated healthcare in several European countries. Some sounded pretty good, but cost-cutting measures are now in demand and operating these systems has and can cause millions in government debt. Some patients say they must fight for some treatments. Others dislike the slow drug approvals. Limits on medical treatments can be at issue, and doctors can be limited in what money they can make per quarter. Some doctors close shop once their limit has been met for the quarter. Nevertheless, all of these systems have been rated higher than America's by most international health care comparisons (see npr.org for more details).

There are cultural differences, too, that affect healthcare expenses and care. In the Netherlands, for example, people believe babies should be born at home. Euthanasia is accepted and legal for people who want to die due to their severe medical condition. Pain medication is looked down upon. These cultural cost savings would never translate to American culture to save money. Regardless, all the top European plans are said to be more cost-effective than ours and they treat everyone. Studying them is worth a second look even though my first reaction is to defend our own broken system. I won't do it, however, since I agree it's a system that needs work (and foreigners hate it when we keep saying how great everything is here).

A missionary who visited our church a few years back spoke about her life in Africa compared to here. She came back shocked at the amount of advertising for facial creams and such in America. There's just no place for that kind of thing with the work and need she faces on her missions projects. Recently more representatives from a children's charity in Africa visited Elsa's church. When the African-born representative "Charles" spoke to the church, he spent some of the time speaking about Elsa. He was astounded that the pastor had just announced to the congregation that Elsa turned 101 a day prior. Before Charles left, he requested photos to be taken with him and this "gorgeous, dressed to kill woman." Of course Elsa gladly obliged. He wanted to inspire the children who were so accustomed to pandemics and other factors currently producing an average lifespan of only 40 years in their area of Malawi. ... And a Peace Corp. volunteer I once met in the late 80's said her travels and experiences were life altering, however her frustration grew in Honduras with women who didn't flinch at their husbands having many lovers, even with the potential for spread of STD's (sexually transmitted diseases). Also, the attempts to keep up sanitary conditions to control sickness was just not accepted by the people there as a priority. Their other needs were too immediate, so thinking of protecting themselves from possible future problems was a hard sell.

So, Elsa is right. It's interesting and enlightening to see the world, exploring and enjoying other cultures. Most love and cherish their native land. Your home country is going to have a love and an understanding that goes both ways to make you prefer it over any other. The United States, however, obviously attracts and welcomes people the world over who relish our opportunity and freedoms here. This is what Elsa so admires and speaks of.

Hopefully this mini-world tour of thoughts, people and places opened your mind to think of how much you love your country. No matter how many years Elsa lives here in America, she appreciates it every day, not taking it for granted. It is part of her happiness to consciously adore America. She doesn't have to agree with every policy of the country to admire what's good.

Despite the perceived politics and problems, America looks better than ever to me, and it's always working to improve. Elsa's patriotism has easily passed down through the generations of our family.

Drink in the Beauty with Your Eyes and Ears

Elsa went with a group of friends and my mom to see famed Dutch violinist and conductor Andre' Reiu conduct an orchestra with a thrilling musical selection. She said she was so enthralled with the performance she felt it energized and electrified her entire being. I know what she's talking about. We should all try to allow these experiences into our lives as much as possible like Elsa does. All I could think of, however, in my own experience, was shortly after I met my husband Mike when we had our first dance at a local hangout where we both lived in New Jersey. I got that "electric" feeling through my torso. I guess it's a shot of adrenalin ...

not exactly the same as Elsa's experience with the orchestra, and possibly with more of a sexual charge to it, but the point is to make space in your life for absorbing beauty in all its' forms, for no other reason or goal than to feel good!

My second thought was of a concert Mike and I attended to see "Bad Company", or whoever originals were left with some new guys. It was a really fun experience and we should go to more concerts of any type. It had been so long since I had been to a "rock" concert that I was a little concerned we would feel out-of-place, but most of the crowd was within Baby Boomer range. Some even passed around the communal joints. The main thing that changed about us since our younger days of concert-going was we worried about what could be in that stuff so prominently potent in our surrounding shared air … and where has that mouth been on the stranger who just puffed it? Needless to say we wanted no part of it. When offered to us, Mike put up his arm like he was an orange belt clad safety patrol boy halting a student from crossing the road. We all accepted each other's preference on the matter and that was it. If only they could see the red-haired-hippie my husband once was. I hardly believed it myself.

So we enjoyed the concert, and did so on our own drugless terms. The same goes for a beautiful landscape (I still recall my 8th grade science teacher telling us nature has a lot of green for a reason; It's very pleasing to the eye), flower, person or array of nicely prepared and displayed food … drink it in, enjoy it, appreciate it. Even watching your team play a sport can be something to drink in. Have you ever watched a South American soccer game and heard the announcer say "goooaaaaaaaal" for a longer amount of time than an American Idol singer's last note in a performance? Now that's someone drinking in some non-liquidated pure pleasure.

Abraham Lincoln loved all kinds of music. In fact, he continued to go to operas during the Civil War and was criticized for doing so. He didn't let that dissuade him, however, as he declared he needed that time for a change of atmosphere. If he made the time for pleasures like the arts, you can, too. Ironically, he always said one of his favorite tunes was "Dixieland" (really).

Keep the Dining Room

Dining with one's friends and beloved family is certainly one of life's primal and most innocent delights, one that is both soul-satisfying and eternal.
Julia Child

Recently I saw on TV that the latest remodeling craze is changing the formal dining room into something else such as an office, a den, a media room, etc. Since our culture has become so casual, many rarely use this room so it has been deemed nonfunctional. As a Jersey girl would say in disbelief, "Get out!" as in "Get out of town" (if that still doesn't make sense, just hang in there with me on this).

Do you know Europeans don't understand how we can woof down food in our cars or eat standing as we catch a favorite program finishing on TV? Often eating is not "dining" here anymore. Other countries (and thin people in general) make eating more of a pleasant ritual meant to savor. Even coffee-to-go is a fairly new concept in other countries. Lidded disposable cups weren't a readily available option in Europe until Starbucks came to England in 1998 (to Tokyo 1996).

Some of my best childhood memories are of family dining room dinners at my parents' or at Elsa's. Elsa would even allow us kids to use exquisite crystal glasses like the grown-ups. She made it special for everyone. Dinner together was important quality family time.

I feel happy Mike and I have been able to cook for her, too, (actually usually Mike cooks and I clean) and we all eat in our dining room. We have enjoyed major holidays together as well as princess birthday parties. Please keep, and use, the dining room.

Respect Other Cultures

Elsa's passion for world travel includes researching and learning about other cultures. It's part of the fun and part of that word I use frequently, "respect" for others. Fortunately world travel often has great deals for the average American to afford. Unfortunately that means you get American jerky people (of many economic statuses) travelling, too, who leave a bad impression of America in their path. I've heard of average Americans in their typical baseball hats and sneakers blowing in the faces of the standing like a statue Royal British guardsmen. Makes ya cringe, doesn't it? And then there are all those American movies with ruthless Russians that made our initial landing in Moscow to visit our adopted children-to-be terrifying until we linked up with our driver and interpreter. I have to tell you, we soon learned the Russians were much, much warmer people than any other foreigners I had ever met. Even when our language differences barred us from having conversation, the women I met at the children's homes (the girls were from two different ones) had a universal kindness recognizable in their eyes and smiles. When I made my Russian phrases attempts, it was appreciated. One Russian-speaking woman at Elsa's children's home practiced her English, too, saying our daughter was a "princess", as she looked adoringly at our little Elsa and back at me smiling. I was very touched and that is one of my most vivid and moving memories of the adventure we had in adopting and traveling there.

At first, many Americans may consider the Russians' business dealings odd. Most payments for the services needed by others to help you adopt (adoption is free or near free, but you need help to do it internationally) need to be made in cash, and the bills need to be clean and defect free or else they are not accepted. We had one bill rejected that we had to have replaced even though our American bank was so careful and helpful to give us the best clean bills they had. They all looked perfect to me. Regardless, when in Rome …, and it was a minor inconvenience to handle when looking at the powerful life changing transition of becoming an instant family about to occur. Who knows why they are so particular, but whether it's a problem with trust or with counterfeit money, it's just their way.

Some people consider their custom of giving a gift to everybody who helps you in an adoption as more like a bribe. I say that's unfounded. It's not mandatory, but it's their way of doing things, just like Americans find it productive to get right down to the beef of a matter immediately in business, but other cultures like to warm up to it with some social niceties first. In Russia, I liked giving people simple gifts like Florida t-shirts and postcards of south Florida manatees and such. They lit up to get them. And as for gifts recommended for the children's homes, we felt great about supplying them with those huge bottles of kid's vitamins you get at those warehouse stores, as well as other things they always are in need of.

A co-worker of mine in the late 1980's had told me about her visit to see relatives in Hungary. She got so tired of cousins asking things like "How many cars do you have?" that she started to answer "One for every day of the week." She was a very nice person, but she became overwhelmed and irritated with the misconceptions many there had of America. No matter how hard she had tried to change their incorrect perceptions, no one would listen. It's true that Americans like to accumulate a lot of "fun stuff", but most work long hours and many years to get these things. Do we overdo it? Yes, we often do, both with work and buying things. However, more than one car per person is not common (at least not from my view of the American pie).

At a South American friend's party in the early 1990's (a traditional celebration with Latin dancing and drinks until dinner was served near midnight) the hosts told me, "We came here to America and worked hard. We have our nice house and business and beautiful pool. We achieved our American dream. Now we are thinking of going back home to Colombia." The "takeaway" here: It can be a tough journey to live out the American dream, especially compared to seemingly simpler and less harried cultures. Not all desire this life we love. Learning to balance it all well can be done, however, if the desire is there. Certainly Elsa is an example of one who has done just that.

A tribe (I believe Aboriginal from Australia) I once read about that still live in the ways of their ancestors, expressed shock at our baby cribs in the modern world. They asked a westerner if it was true we put our babies in "those cages." This brings to light that it's important to realize our ways are not the only ways or even the best ways, and to keep our minds open to other cultural views.

That seems to be a big problem with the lack of American popularity out there in rest of the world. We don't understand how vastly different other cultures may think and we don't do enough research and PR to bridge the gap so we can understand each other better (and vice versa). There are some shocking spewing blood cartoons of our political leaders seen as normal humor in some Arab countries. I don't get it, but there's such a great divide in our understanding of each other that I am not angry. I am just sad about it, and praying for a breakthrough in shared communication and understanding.

Elsa has always instilled in us an appreciation of our own heritage with taking us to German and American cultural events as children and telling us about how her parents persisted to be successful and to be American. She also respects and enjoys other cultures, whether it is on a trip or in an ethnic restaurant locally. Having this open mind to the way other people and cultures are different I believe is another key to her positive aging. Her example helps us bridge the gap, one person at a time, between the misunderstandings among cultures, and allows for the enjoyment of our differences.

Go with the Light

Alas, this is not about the afterlife. This is about safety. Actually my paternal grandmother, Ruth Textor aka "Nanna", who died while I was in college, always used to say this for "Better safe than sorry driving." I go to the exit with a traffic light when exiting a store or main road even when it seems absolutely unnecessary and looks much quicker to go to a non-light crossover or exit.

One never knows, and Elsa also realizes the importance of safety when driving or for anything else (ok, except for her stove malfunction caused by a pen falling into one of the burners which has since been averted with a new glass top stove; it could have happened to anyone with a busy social calendar hung in a cabinet near the scene of the incident).

Being safe means sometimes saying no to your pride. One of Elsa's friends, who has since passed on, once told me he hated the fact he had to use a walker to get around. I tried to get him to see that without using it he was in a far more possible situation of falling and humiliating himself and he should try to be happy he had a means of walking. I don't know if that helped, but in comparison, Elsa now uses a cane. She wasn't instantly thrilled with the idea, but has since made lemons out of lemonade by using a cane as a fashion accessory. Elsa now collects canes to match her outfits (She took five of them with her on her latest cruise, even lending one to a friend). Elsa designed one cane by having it covered with the same material matching perfectly to her exquisite 100th birthday party outfit. How original and elegant!

Elsa's neighbors watch out for each other. That's part of a good safety plan. When one of the neighbors saw me when I lived in the same building, she told me it looked like Elsa had left one of her canes by the elevator. Now a stranger may have been worried that something may have happened to a 100 year old whose cane was found by the elevator. Nevertheless, neither the neighbor nor I were alarmed. We knew Elsa likely had her hands full of groceries or a plant or something and left the cane behind. That's not exactly a good example of Elsa acting in the safest way, but this story does convey people know she is strong and determined. Because Elsa is in such good physical shape, it shifts our perceptions of what we know a centenarian like her is capable of doing.

When travelling, she has a fold-up wheel chair if needed for rough seas or long distances across a cruise ship or for an afternoon shore tour. Of course it has her initials beautifully embroidered in gold on the back of the chair. Safety doesn't have to be boring!

When I used to work in a large company, I got to go to one of those seminars Disney puts on for managers (known as a vacation day to most!). One of the managers at my circular table was from a local grocery store chain. He was adamant about one of the answers we were all trying to find agreement on regarding the top five things (in order from most important to least) that any company , no matter what size, should prioritize.

I had been in corporate America long enough to know that every time we got a new head honcho there would be a new priority ... put the employees on teams to make company policy ... dissolution of the teams because they are taking too long and don't know what they are doing ... set strict rules: management is in charge ... ease the rules: happy employees work harder ... acknowledge those who have been loyal to the company ... make the long-term loyal employees re-apply for their jobs at a lower wage or take a severance package ... insist on a degree for promotions ... relax the degree prerequisite for promotions ... yada yada yada blah blah blah .... So was company profit first? Productivity? Retaining employees? Eliminating employees? Rewarding employees? Cleanliness? Customer Satisfaction? Career Path Planning? As we argued over these as to what the most important was, the grocery store guy said, "Trust me. It's safety."

We all thought this guy was way out of the loop. Yet he was right. Whether you are the corner store (are there any of them anymore?), an individual, a family, or Disney World, safety is first. It makes sense once you clear your head out of all that rote corporate training and re-training and actually read those safety signs posted in the warehouses.

Try New Things - We Have the Technology

Elsa was born way before many of our current modern conveniences were the norm. Horse and buggy was still a major form of everyday family transportation (and not everyone could do it well; Elsa's husband Bill was known for being the best in his family at it). Microwaves and cell phones weren't invented until she was well into her senior years. In the newspaper Elsa was given from the year she was born, a report was on carrier pigeons used for baseball game updates (every 10 minutes) because the telegraph employees were on strike!

Elsa also recalls milk, ice and beer deliveries as a child. Milk was served out of a ladle from a metal container in the ice box once in house. Beer barrels were rolled into place to a tavern neighboring their family bakery. Elsa remembers that beer was made at home during the Prohibition Era (1920-1933; Prohibition occurred in several countries around the same time, including Russia). The ingredients were readily available from the local grocery. The authorities were not concerned with home brewed beer for home consumption, but with those trying to sell it. Growing up in a good-sized town (Yonkers), Elsa also recalls and likes to make it clear she wasn't schooled in a one room school house. It was a bigger school, and with large classrooms. She has said "I wasn't out in The Wild West, you know!"

Nevertheless, Elsa tries the new things she thinks she can use, and doesn't cave into the pressures to get things everyone seems to have but she can just as well do without. She relies on a microwave just as much as anyone and she has a cell phone. Regardless, I don't think she'll have an interest in the Google cell phone software that will help you organize your clothes.

Elsa is not running out to learn and buy every technical advance that is popular, but a little while after the Internet was invented, she asked me to show her how it worked. She gave me some things to "Google" and then declared, "That's not so great. You still have to look through all those matches to find what I am looking for? I can get the answer faster the old fashioned way of making a call or two." So there you have it … some people actually can live successfully in the modern world without being addicted to email, googling and texting just because as a "Six Million Dollar Man" fan or Trekkie would say, "We have the technology." Of course the Internet is invaluable to most (I also do look up information for Elsa on occasion per her request, so she uses it through me and others; Elsa has many senior and younger friends who are computer literate), but the people interaction Elsa often relies on to get her answers is something we should consider sometimes, too, as our "new thing."

No Fear

One who fears failure limits his activities. Failure is only the opportunity to more intelligently begin again.
Henry Ford

The greatest mistake you can make in life is to continually be afraid you will make one.
Elbert Hubbard, American writer, 1856-1915

This topic may make you imagine Elsa taking on the current champion of the American Women's Senior Wrestling Federation (not that this even exists), but I'm going somewhere else here. Confidence is important to a good life. I always admired Elsa's confidence in dealing with people of any social status or cultural background. She gives everyone the benefit of the doubt that their positive light will show if they are treated with cheer and respect. In the unlikely event that the response from someone is toxic, she just moves on. It's their problem, but hopefully her kindness will help them react better to the next person in their path.

This philosophy of treating others well has bid her well in acquiring a huge group of friends and aids in how she gets tasks accomplished. Having this history of positive living in how she treats others has given her a flowing resume of holding wonderful and memorable gatherings. This gives her the fearless drive to do more, like being the main planner, per her choice, of her 100th birthday party given to her by her children. No detail was forgotten. She used her creative flair and expertise selecting the invitations, menu, guest list, seating, color scheme, favors, venue selection and personally addressing the invitations for a gala of nearly 200 guests.

Elsa continues to "have no fear" and maintain healthy confidence at over 100 years old. Recently it took guts for her to say yes to being raffled off as a dinner date for a charity raffle. In addition, at over 100 years young, she started a new exercise regimen to attain more strength to get out of her bubble baths. It is also noteworthy that in her 80's, Elsa had two knee replacements done simultaneously. She worked diligently adhering to the exercising advised by her doctor. After she healed, she played the best golf game of her life.

If Elsa has a bad day, she says she just puts on her lipstick and gets on with it with what's next. From a t-shirt I saw in a magazine, I use a phrase with similar meaning to push myself and others on, "Get on your big girl panties and deal with it." (For men, "Get on your big boy pants and deal with it.")

Talking about strength (as in motivation to action beyond confidence), when Elsa's husband Bill was getting terribly sick with bronchitis every winter, Elsa knew she needed a plan for his health. That's when they started visiting south Florida seasonally in the 1930's. It was not very built up then. They initially traveled by ship from New York to south Florida with their two young children. Elsa's friends told her it was too primitive in Florida and there would be no milk for her baby. Regardless, she felt it was the best plan for her husband's health and she made the plans. Bill felt better after one or two days in the Florida sun and the sea air.

Elsa loved the fragrance of the flowers when they arrived and was enchanted by Florida's tropical glory. However, when it came time to finding accommodations, it was easier to find a place allowing pets than a couple with a baby. Elsa recalls Bill would set up the family comfortably at the beach while he looked for a place to stay. Elsa has always made it known that it was a lovely Jewish lady who ultimately allowed this young family to rent a room at her accommodations. The lady's children were older, and she would volunteer to babysit Elsa and Bill's children so Elsa and Bill could catch a break and go for daily walks together. Elsa says the woman and her family were a delight.

Eventually, by the 1950's, they bought their own place in Pompano Beach which was a group of eight apartments. In five years, they transformed it into a larger thirty-eight unit motel resort. They were pioneers in Pompano because before the motels came in the 50's, the area was mainly agricultural. The motel operators helped popularize the area for tourism. Bill and Elsa owned and managed the resort for about twenty winter seasons. They had no previous experience in the resort business. The Hoffmann's believed that people should have a good time on their vacation. They created a popular resort with their house party style venture.

Elsa says the motel resort was accomplished not only with passion and investment from her husband and herself, but with the dedicated assistance of employees that would get things set up while Elsa and Bill were still up in New York. In addition, they had an architect whom they had full faith in to complete projects while they were up north in the summers. His name is Robert Todd.

Robert Todd read an article about Elsa in 2007. He looked her up and invited her to his home in John Knox Village in Pompano, Florida, a popular retirement community for active seniors. Todd and his wife Helen welcomed Elsa and Elsa's daughter Joan into their home to reminisce about Jasmin Villa. It was his pleasure to work on the motel and he recalls the great trust the Hoffmann's put in him as the design was implemented. Mr. Todd remembers it was the loveliest motel in the area at the time. He still has the original architectural drawings of the plans.

Robert Todd said that in 1954 he opened Todd and Wiesman Architects in Pompano Beach with his friend George Wiesman. Robert noted that he and partner George were members of the American Institute of Architects.

In addition to Jasmin Villa, a favorite commission for him was designing the famous Pier 66 icon tower in Fort Lauderdale. He explained that the original design of the tower was adapted by Phillips Petroleum. The current owner of the luxury hotel and marina complex, Hyatt Regency, explains further history on their website. They state that the original vision by Phillips was for a watercraft fueling station. Elsa and Bill were referred to Todd and Wiesman by New York friends.

Elsa had gotten her penchant for remodeling apartments back during The Great Depression. She and her husband lived in an apartment building they owned. In order to help people and to become profitable enough to hang on to the building, they made the apartments smaller so they were more affordable to people at that difficult financial time and could hold more people. A government program, in addition to their own funds, made this desirable and possible. It worked out well for all involved. Elsa was "thinking outside of the box", and that's exactly the best description of how she operates.

Elsa did not hesitate (nor have any fear) when my six year old daughter Blair wanted her to come visit her school. Blair's friends did not believe her that she had a healthy, active and pretty great-grandmother that was over 100 years old. Some would take pause before addressing a group of first and second graders, regardless of their own age, but Elsa welcomed the exchange.

As my mother Joan, Elsa and I entered the room, we saw three chairs nicely set up for us at the head of the class. Elsa purposely disregarded the rocking chair (My mom used it!). She ended up standing speaking to the children for over an hour because all were so engaged in the presentation. Elsa spoke of being kind to others and respect for teachers. She also shared photos of her world travels and a laminated newspaper from her birth date. The fashion and baseball pages caught the children's eyes from the paper, as well as Elsa's India travel photos posing with elephants.

The children had questions, such as "Was there fast food when you were young?" Elsa replied "Oh no, but my parents had a bakery, so I was always popular. Children could come with me after school to pick out a treat." When I asked the class, "How do you think someone lives this long and is so healthy at 100 years old?" One boy raised his hand high and responded quite seriously, "With pills." Although that was funny, if these youngsters think that's the big secret, we have a lot more work to do!

Do you know what gerontophobia is? You can probably figure it out (fear of aging), but I didn't even know this term existed until I was researching types of lesson plans on positive aging that may be of interest to my daughters' school. There are oodles of websites that cover this real fear many people have. What a waste of happiness and energy to live this way. Please seek help if this is your reality. Learn to embrace and welcome that AARP membership application that will track you down like a dog on your 50th birthday! Take advantage of the senior discounts for movies and all kinds of attractions in your own towns and beyond. Feel well and be well as you age.

Elsa looks at her life as the amazing ride it has been and continues to be, concentrating on what is beautiful and not fearing if this is her last day or if there are many years ahead for her. When she was on a cruise where some got ill, she did not panic. She enjoyed her trip, taking precautions to stay well. When Elsa and Joan went on a trip to the British Isles, their plane was the last to land before flights were all held due to a terrorist scare in 2006 at Heathrow Airport. They were assured they were safe for their cruise, so they had a blast without fear.

On those days that I am feeling overwhelmed or fearful of the future, I think about the wonderful family I have and our closeness to my mother and grandmother, as well as all the joyful times past and dreams to come. There's always something you can remember with love. You can always find something to look forward to or to plan. There's always something you can enjoy right now. Make the attitude shift yourself as needed so as not to live with regret on your deathbed that you didn't do something important because of fear, or lived unhappily due to a bad attitude.

Life Interrupted - The Big Vacation

Stress is one of the biggest complaints of Baby Boomers, yet studies have been done that say each generation has dealt with stress, way back to the cavemen stressed out on where to track down their next meal for their families and tribe. It's hard to believe stress isn't worse now, though, as we absorb more information daily than ever before. We feel we must multi-task and we're often preoccupied with our to-do lists. One of our supplier delivery people, Lucius, told us he can see from his truck height people who have left coffee and cell phones on their car roofs as they drive on the main roads. He says he sees this often. I say this is one small, yet sure sign that we need to balance our lives more. We're rushing and stressing too much.

Elsa has not been immune to stress. Years of learning how to handle life's adversities has taught her when to accept, when to try to change circumstances, and/or to pray on it (kind of like the AA serenity prayer).

She also uses the yoga technique of relaxing each part of her body one part at a time. I sometimes use that to relax and get to sleep, but being a Baby Boomer who would rather just take a pill, I unfortunately often do that instead (often homeopathic, though!). Now that I've taken the time to think and write about it, however, it has revived my goal to do the yoga thing more often.

Nevertheless, Elsa is the first to admit that the pressures of being a young bride (married in 1926 at age 18), starting a family, and helping with family business bookkeeping got to her as she tried to balance it all. It was too much and she took "the big vacation" around the late 1920's. The recuperation period after her nervous breakdown got her back on track to organizing her priorities, living positively every day, and not trying to do more than is humanly possible. Today we have Lexapro (or something similar). Don't deny it. Many a busy Baby Boomer pre-, peri- or in menopause mom has found it helpful.

Elsa has a regular housecleaner to help her keep her condo in its usual spotless condition. It's not that expensive, at least not here in south Florida. Daughter Pamela often stops by to help if needed, too.

I enjoy cleaning and organizing, but when there's just no time with all the other priorities we create for ourselves and our families, I have also welcomed the assistance of a housecleaner myself. When I visited my friend's home in Colombia, there was help all over the place. There was someone to get your Coca Cola at the house, someone who did the ironing, the cleaning, and the errands (even for a relatively small home/condo). Perhaps we don't need all that, and our economy is much different, anyway. We still have a middle class (I think). Regardless, paying for getting some help here and there (housecleaner, organizer, caterer, babysitter, seamstress, life coach, spirituality seminar, etc.) instead of a night out may be just what you need. **Asking for help when you need it is not weak. It's smart.**

Elsa with seven of her great-grandchildren at a beach barbecue celebrating a weekend of her 99th birthday festivities, 2006.

Elsa with daughter Joan, great-grandchildren Blair, age 5, and Elsa, age 3; Elsa won a prize for her scarecrow outfit at the Deerfield Country Club Party that night, 10/2006.

Elsa, at age 100, with historian Bud Garner, on the 2007 lead boat "The Musette" during the Pompano Beach Holiday Boat Parade. Elsa is displaying Bud's work entitled "Tales of Old Pompano."

While on the boat, Pompano's theme song, "Florida's Pompano Beach", was played. Elsa and family are honored to know Bill "Clancy" Jaycox who wrote the song. His song was named the "Official Song of Pompano" and Clancy was named "Official City Song Writer" by the Pompano Beach Commissioners.

Clancy and his wife Joanne are also involved with various charitable endeavors, including their well-known holiday stints as Mr. and Mrs. Santa Claus. Additionally, Joanne is an active member in QUOTA.

Elsa on one of her trips, seen with face circled; at famous
Tiger Tops Jungle Lodge in India.

Elsa with a Ladies Club, at the Stork Club, NY, NY; Elsa is to the back right.

Elsa, husband Bill, daughter Joan and her husband Richard, grandchildren Christine, Richard, and Sharon, at Fort Lauderdale Sheraton for dinner and ice show; late1960's. (Elsa and author Sharon, front right)

Mardi Gras Party, 1976; Elsa as Madam Pompadour, with Bill as one of the lords; Elsa had just gotten her facelift done a few months before and was ready to party again!

Elsa singing at the piano as Bill plays beautiful music; Besides being a
wonderful pianist and successful businessman, Bill was a Rotarian in Mount
Vernon, New York. He and Elsa would delight in bringing back international
banners from Rotarian groups they had visited on their trips as was tradition.
Elsa was called a "Rotary Ann", a name that evolved from a woman named
Ann that accompanied her husband on a train ride to a Rotarian convention
in 1914. She was the only woman on the train for most of the trip, and then
the name stuck (until the 1980's), especially after they met another couple at
the convention with the wife named Ann (see rotaryfirst100.org). In addition
to supporting her husband's community efforts through the Rotary, while
in New York Elsa was in charitable groups such as one that supported local
hospitals.

Elsa and Bill were members of The Westchester Country Club when they
lived in Mount Vernon and later in Rye, NY. They had joined because
they felt it was a perfect place for family celebratory get-togethers. The
club has a beach club on Manursing Island, also in Rye. The author recalls
many cherished memories of her youth and young adulthood connected to
family gatherings at these places. Elsa and Bill received the added benefit
of marvelous lifelong friendships cultivated there. In addition, Elsa was a
scorekeeper several times at PGA tournaments held at the club yearly in
June's great weather. Each player had their own scorekeeper that followed
them on the course. Elsa recalls, "All of us (scorekeeper women) had cute
matching uniforms." (Boomer recollection: my little brother Richard collected
autographs from the pros at the putting green in the 60's)

Bathing beauties Elsa (left) and younger sister Gretchen, 1924.

Elsa and Bill on a camping excursion.

Christmastime in Georgia with great-grandchildren Catherine and Will, 2002.

California and Colorado relatives celebrate the weekend of Elsa's 100th birthday, seen here at the famous award winning SeaWatch Restaurant, Ft. Lauderdale, FL. The families shown represent The DeLong's of Pueblo, Colorado, The Pyle's of Poway, California, and The Jacques' of Covina, California.

Ceremony at First Presbyterian Church, Pompano, FL, for their Lighthouse Christian School building addition; Elsa and friend Dottie Jones were honored as the ribbon-cutters, 2008.

Elsa and her children Joan Marie Textor, Gail E. Hoffmann, and Pamela Elsa Hoffmann; Elsa's 101st birthday, 10/2008.

Elsa's "Medical and Spiritual Advisors", Dr. John Strobis and Rev. Dr. Jack Noble, at Elsa's 95th birthday.

Attending a Northeast FOCAL Point charitable event at Deerfield Country Club, Deerfield Beach, FL; Joan Textor, Mayor of Hillsboro Beach Carmen McGarry, Duane Timm, Elsa (2008). Northeast FOCAL Point provides a full spectrum of services for elders, administered by The City of Deerfield Beach. Elsa is a member of this organization.

Elsa clowns around at church celebration of new school building, 2008; church friend Deacon Earl Harris is to the right.

Elsa poses with enthusiastic children after her presentation to 1st and 2nd graders at SeaWind Elementary School, Hobe Sound, FL, 2008.

Elsa, Barbara, Joan at Elsa's N.Y. interview for the show: "How to Live to 150 - Can You Do It?" which aired in April 2008. Four other noteworthy centenarians were also in the project.

Elsa receives a proclamation from Deerfield Beach, Florida, presented by Mayor Capellini. It was awarded for her positive aging and living example, as well as her involvement and support for local charitable organizations. She also received proclamations from Hillsboro Beach on her 95th and 100th birthdays.

Oktoberfest Party at Elsa and Bill's home in Rye, NY; Bill with daughters Joan (left) and Pamela; 1960's; Elsa cooked the German dinner food consisting of sauerbraten and more for 125 guests.

Oktoberfest party at Elsa and Bill's home in Rye, NY, 1960's; Elsa with
guests (Elsa second from right). Elsa and Bill had a finished basement
with an extra kitchen just for events such as this in her Rye, NY home.
Of additional interest: Yes, Oktoberfest is about celebration, music, friends,
and beer, but there is much more in the history. It originated as a horserace in
Bavaria honoring the marriage of Crown Prince Ludwig and Therese in 1810;
The celebration continued yearly and evolved over the years worldwide,
only being cancelled in Germany during times of war and cholera; the
spiked helmet on one of the guests above was a style originated in 1800's
Prussia as indicated by the single-headed eagle emblem; Russia originated it
at the same time with a 2-headed eagle emblem; many countries followed
suit with spiked helmets all the way to South America; Later it proved to
be too cumbersome for combat and was used for ceremonial military garb,
ceasing to be part of German uniforms by 1918, but still used in Sweden and
Colombia, for example, for ceremonial use and parades; In 2006, during the
lead-up to the FIFA World Cup Soccer Tournament in Germany, a plastic
replica of the spike helmet was made in German flag colors
for fan memorabilia. It did not sell well! (from answers.com for Pickelhaube
information)

Elsa posing with the new car she got herself for her 100th birthday! Local Forum newspapers staff writer, Elizabeth Roberts, said "It takes optimism to buy a new car for your 100th birthday. It takes chutzpah to drive it, but Elsa has plenty of both."

The cruise group from Deerfield Country Club; Elsa and Joan near front, January 2008, Caribbean Cruise.

Baby Elsa with older brother Hugo

Elsa recalls milk, ice and beer deliveries as a young child (OK, yes, as a Boomer we had a milk delivery man, too, when I was a kid in the 60's. Do you remember those returnable glass bottles?). She does not recall clearly the transition of the deliveries from horse drawn carriage to auto (as a time/history reference, however, The Yonkers Fire Department bought their first motorized pumping fire engine in 1910 when Elsa was 3, but wasn't fully motorized/horse-free until 1916; see yfd.org/history), but she has other interesting recollections. Milk was served out of a ladle from a metal container in the ice box. Ice boxes (in 1908, for example, sold at Sears for $7 to $18, which was a lot of money at the time) had to be drained daily and replaced with new ice deliveries at least a few times a week (coincidently, I recently learned that my dad, at age 13 in the mid-1940's, was an ice delivery boy in the country of northwestern NJ! The police let him drive without a license early in the mornings because the service was a necessity; The more I hear about family history, the more amazing it is to think of all Elsa has seen for over 100 years ... and the more lucky we appear to be with all our modern conveniences). Beer barrels were rolled into place at a tavern neighboring their family bakery. Growing up in a good-sized town (Yonkers), she does like to make it clear that she wasn't in a one room school house when she was school-age. It was a bigger school, and with large classrooms. She has said "I wasn't out in 'The Wild West', you know!"

Just imagine, in 1907 when Elsa was born:

➢ Theodore Roosevelt was President

➢ Oklahoma became the 46th state

➢ John D. Rockefeller upgrades from a horse drawn carriage to an automobile

➢ Horses sold from $150 to $300 each

➢ Cars sold for an average $500 (the high was $2800)

➢ Gas was 6 cents a gallon, bread 5 cents, stamps 2 cents

➢ The Cubs won the World Series against the Tigers, 4-0

➢ The Great White Fleet, consisting of 16 battleships and 12,000 men, began a round-the-world cruise to convince the world of the U.S. being a major naval power.

➢ Mark Twain receives an honorary doctorate degree at Oxford (he lived until 1910)

➢ San Francisco had an outbreak of the plague (affected 52 countries)

➢ Polio was a widespread problem – 1000 die in NY

➢ The first electric ball drops in Times Square

➢ The average yearly income in the U.S. is under $900

➢ Doctors had little proper training available until well into the 1930's; prior to readily available doctors (in the early 1900's and prior), the main people tending to the sick often included mothers, ministers, and barber-surgeons; almost all births took place at home until the 1920's; barber-surgeons conducted tooth extractions and minor surgeries, including cataract removal until the late 1800's (barber-surgeon history reveals the red, blue and white barber pole origin: to symbolize the bloodletting procedures they once did! Bloodletting procedures stopped in the early 1900's). As substandard medical schools and diploma mills were weeded out, the number of medical schools dropped from 160 in 1904 to 66 in 1935 (also helped along by the 1910 Flexner Report recommendations). Elsa was born during a time of big and positive changes emerging for proper patient care.

➤ The first practical telephone, although invented in 1876, did not become widely available in America until the early 1900's; many contributed to the earlier research and others claimed to have invented it first, but Alexander Graham Bell was the first to patent it; Bell's main interest was working on hearing devices which lead to this accidental phone discovery; his mother and wife were deaf; He later made groundbreaking discoveries in hydrofoils and aeronautics; in 1888 he became one of the founding members of The National Geographic Society. (Boomer recollections: My husband recalls needing the operator to make calls during the 1950's in Pompton Lakes, NJ; I recall "party lines" in our rural northwestern NJ town in the 1960's where you had to wait for neighbors to finish their calls before you could make a call.)

➤ Electricity, originally harnessed in 1821, was not readily accessible to the general public in America until 1880-1920.

- Others born in 1907:
- Barbara Stanwyck (d. 1990)
- John Wayne (d. 1979)
- Katharine Hepburn (d. 2003)
- Sir Laurence Olivier (d. 1989)
- James A. Michener (d. 1997)

(numerous sources contain parts or all of the above information, including history1900s.about.com, npr.org, wikepedia.org, medicinenet.com, jama. ama-assn.org, pewresearch.org)

Elsa and Bill on the grounds of their Jasmin Villa resort in Pompano Beach, FL. that they owned and operated seasonally from the 1950's for about 20 years.

This photo was in the newspaper when Elsa's first granddaughter Christine was born. It said:

Heirloom Christening

The gown is worn by Christine Marie Textor, pictured in the arms of her great-grandmother, Mrs. Otto Brehm of Yonkers. The gown, made by Mrs. Brehm, was also worn by Christine's grandmother, Mrs. William Hoffmann of 39 Alta Drive, standing, and by the infant's mother, Mrs. Richard Textor of Sussex, NJ, the former Joan Hoffmann, also shown. The infant's four grandparents and her four maternal great-grandparents were present for her christening.

Elsa, at age 100, gambles and enjoys some party libations with daughter Joan and wonderful friends Lucy Bergman (standing left), and Terry Nanry (sitting right). They were celebrating "Kentucky Derby Day" at Deerfield Country Club. Elsa won on her bets as well as first prize in the decorated derby theme hat contest.

Elsa and Bill in their Mount Vernon, NY home, for a family celebration (late 1950's). Elsa is presenting the cake.

Elsa the bride, June 1926.

Elsa and Bill actively having fun as always; seen here with son
William "Buddy" (late 1920's).

Seven of Elsa's great-grandchildren at her 100th birthday gala. She likes to see
the men as well as the boys in jacket and tie. They look great, don't they?
Back: Catherine, Will and Elliot Textor of Huntsville, Alabama; Zachary and
Pamela VonOesen, Sussex, NJ Front: Blair and Elsa Textor-Black,
Hobe Sound, FL

Youngest great-grandchild Brooklyn Hoffmann with mom April (2008).

A celebratory toast at Elsa's 100th birthday. Elsa is at the head table with her children. Long-standing friend Joan Daly, Founder of the Boca Habilitation Center (standing) is seen to the right of the head table. She is a friend Elsa has known since they were members of the Westchester County Club in Rye, NY.

Family at Elsa's 95th birthday party, held at Deerfield Country Club, Deerfield Beach, FL: Daughter Pamela Elsa, Elsa's late daughter-in-law Florine (wife of Gail), nephew Ernie Brehm Jr., and granddaughter Sharon Elsa

Elsa with Countess Henrietta de Hoernle and Flossy Keesley, both who are among her long-standing friends; The event was The American Music Celebration & Reception, by Boca Raton Philharmonic Symphonia, at The Count de Hoernle Amphitheater, April 2008 .

Elsa and Bill met Rita and her husband Adolph during a world travel tour, then becoming great friends getting together for social and family get-togethers over the years. The Countess and her late husband, Count Adolph de Hoernle, became avid supporters of the Boca Raton Community and outlying areas. They contributed to over 140 organizations from hospitals to colleges and more. The Countess continues the charitable work.

Floss also has had and continues to have an interesting and charitable life. She met Elsa in Rye, NY, through the Westchester Country Club. As the wife of the late TV producer and director Nicholas Keesely, Floss came to know famous folks like Arthur Godfrey, Ed Sullivan and Jackie Gleason personally. She has qualified for membership in the PYRAMID Legacy Society with estate gift provisions for The Cleveland Clinic in memory of her husband. In addition, among other charitable gifts, she donated $200,000 for a beautiful fountain at the "Pathway to the Stars" entrance to the Count de Hoernle Amphitheater in Boca Raton, FL. Floss is working on a show about happy themes to lift people up; Elsa was taped as an interviewed guest for the pilot.

Elsa with her late son William "Bud" F. Hoffmann. "My firstborn died - but love is forever." Buddy's wife was the late Joan Marie Hoffmann (yes, the name caused a lot of fun confusion over the years with Elsa's daughter's name, Joan Marie Hoffmann Textor) . They had three children: Bill, Teri and Nancy. Teri and husband Jerry have two handsome boys, Elsa's great-grandchildren Gerald and Billy. Bill's wife's name is Kelli. They have adult children through Kelli's first marriage.

Elsa with long-standing friend Karin Olsen known since Westchester Club days in NY, (interestingly, Karin holds many medals from several countries she earned for the sport of curling), and international entertainer and singer, Doug Crosby, who sang for Elsa at both her 95th and 100th birthday parties.

Many of Elsa's great-grandchildren and great-great-nieces and nephews at her 100th birthday; Two children are named Elsa, a great-granddaughter in Florida and a great-great-niece from California. Children attending were from Massachusetts, California, New Jersey, Connecticut., Colorado, Alabama, Georgia and Florida.

Elsa with her neighbors and dear friends at a Hillsboro Women's League
charitable event, 2008; left to right: Betty Brown, Leatrice Messer, Peg
Hatfield, Elsa, Audrey Pearson

The wedding day of Elsa's first grandchild, Christine Textor VonOesen
(Joan's first child) left to right, Elsa with daughter Joan and family, Cathy
(Richard's pregnant wife who is next to their daughter Catherine), Richard
Textor, Joan, Sharon (sitting), Richard Textor (Sr.), Christine. Richard Sr. is

since deceased. He is buried at Arlington Cemetery in honor of his service during the Korean War.

Bride Christine wore the same veil that her grandmother Elsa and her mother Joan wore on their wedding days. Other granddaughters also carried on this tradition. When Christine was about to get married, Elsa looked for a drycleaner to freshen up the 1926 veil, however none would touch it. Elsa gently hand-washed it herself and it came out beautifully.

Elsa's niece Geraldine Brehm Blair and her brother, Elsa's nephew Richard Brehm, at Geri's daughter Julene's wedding.

Elsa and Bill shipboard with son Buddy and daughter Joan

Although this excursion was not their first trip to Florida and may have been elsewhere, it reminds Elsa of the first ship trip she took with family to Florida when Buddy was a toddler and Joan less than five months old. Elsa loved the fragrance of the flowers when they arrived in Florida, enchanted by Florida's tropical glory. However, when it came time to finding accommodations, it was easier to find a place allowing pets than a couple with small children.

Elsa recalls Bill would set up the family comfortably at the beach while he looked for a place to stay. Elsa has always made it known that it was a nice Jewish lady who ultimately rented accommodations to this young family. The lady's children were older, and she would volunteer to babysit Elsa and Bill's children so Elsa and Bill could go for daily walks together. The owner's teenage children would join them. The walks often included some dancing and singing. Elsa recalls "They were a wonderful family."

After the trip via ship, Elsa recalls on subsequent visits the family drove by a station wagon family car. The Hoffmann's nicknamed their car "The Floridadirondack" since Elsa and Bill loved both north and south … The Adirondacks and Florida. This nickname was painted in gold lettering on the car.

Car travel to Florida brings back memories for Elsa of old wooden bridges that revealed prior damage from floods and hurricanes. What an adventure for the family on these early roads! On the trip down from New York, truck stops served food right to you at your car. The family found it safer and comforting to be near the friendly truck drivers. The Hoffmann's drove at night to avoid traffic. Seeing the scenery and dirt color change from area to area was a beautiful and interesting view. The family admired both small towns and southern cities.

Excitement grew as south Florida neared. Oranges and grapefruit scent could be detected from big trucks transporting the fresh fruit. Spanish moss hung from the trees starting in Georgia. When the town of Stuart, Florida and flowing palms were seen, it was the entryway to south Florida (you know the palm trees in north Florida were planted for the sake of tourism, right? They don't grow quite so naturally there; I learned that at a Disney business seminar!)

Christmastime; Elsa, Bill and children, from oldest to youngest: Buddy, Joan, Gail, Pamela

Granddaughter Sharon Elsa addresses the near 200 guests at Elsa's 100th birthday. Friend and Master of Ceremonies Duane Timm is to the left.

Sharon and husband Mike enjoy Elsa's 100th birthday gala. An ABC cameraman is seen to the right. Family member Dee is seen smiling on the left.

Family from several states gather at a condo community room to view a video of Elsa's life, made by Elsa's niece Geraldine; 2007. Elsa's grandson Craig Hoffmann is running the show (Gail's son). His wife is April, children are adorable girls Charlie and Brooklyn (not shown here). They hail from Georgia. Craig's sister Madeline Cattell is in the background, married to Jim. They have two handsome boys, Justin and Robert, and live in Massachusetts.

Elsa reading the card and enjoying the 100 roses sent by her friends at The Hillsboro Women's League on her 100th birthday; The Hillsboro Women's League, a very lovely and charitable group of woman aged from early 30's and up, named Elsa as their "American Idol" on her 100th!

First Presbyterian Church of Pompano Beach, FL; Elsa is joined by (left to right) Choir Member Ed Hall, Elsa, Charles from Global Missions that the church supports out of Malawi, Africa, for community based orphan care, Rosemarie Stadelman, Missions Committee and Deacon. Charles was amazed by Elsa's looks and health on her 101st birthday that weekend, 10/2008, whereas the average lifespan in his homeland is only 40 years.

Elsa's parents on their wedding day, 1904, Otto and Gretchen Brehm

Elsa and family, late 1930's, Eastertime, Mt. Vernon, NY.

Elsa and Bill canoeing in Lake George, NY.

Cruise Costume party - Elsa as a belly dancer with friends

Elsa with Lighthouse Point, FL Mayor Fred Schorr, at church school building groundbreaking, First Presbyterian Church, Pompano Beach (2007)

Elsa with Pompano Beach Mayor Lamar Fisher, church school building groundbreaking (2007)

Deerfield Country Club golf outing where social members teamed up with golf members; social members did the putting; Elsa with golf buddy Debbie Wilson, the Women's Golf Champion at the club, 2008.

Hawaiian themed party, Elsa with her party girl daughter Joan, 2008

Elsa at her friends' the Tarrent's of Hillsboro Beach, FL; Key West style party; 2008; photo courtesy of Marsha Milot

Architect Robert Todd reunites and reminisces with Elsa about working together on the Jasmin Villa motel resort project more than 50 years prior. He and his wife had invited Elsa and her daughter Joan to their home; he still had the Jasmin Villa plans.

Night at the Races; Elsa was on the social committee at the condominium complex where she lives; estimated 1970's; Pompano Race Track; traditionally a race was named after visiting groups and then photos were taken such as this one with the group's representatives. Elsa is seen to the far right.

91

Elsa on one of her trips; seen here in Greece.

Elsa with friends at Deerfield Country Club when
Elsa received an Appreciation Proclamation and
Honorary Lifetime Membership for her 100th Birthday.
Back left to right: Jean Viola, Jill Radford
Front left to right: Joanne Swensen, Elsa, Rose Poplawsky

Elsa is the first person to prioritize respect for people and other cultures,
however even the best intentions can sometimes go awry ... Although this
photo is fuzzy, it was a moment worth including. Daughter Joan was on a
Balkans trip with Elsa in the 1980's. This photo was taken in a Romanian

castle. Joan suggested that Elsa stand next to the suit of armor. As Elsa went to link her arm around the armor arm, she accidentally pulled the arm out of the socket. Joan was no help as she doubled over in laughter. Elsa tried to fix it, and then said "Just take the picture, Joan" as she balanced the arm into place. A castle employee was quick to come over and calmly resolved the matter.

Another memorable moment on their trip together was visiting the Medjugorie Parish in Bosnia Herzegovina. As throngs of people entered the sacred grounds where visions of the Blessed Virgin Mary had started in 1981, Joan realized one of her contacts had popped out. When Elsa and Joan tried to look around for it without being trampled, Joan discovered it had been captured by her own cleavage. Elsa, in all sincerity, proclaimed more than a little loudly, "It's a miracle! It's a miracle!" Although we all had a bit of a laugh about that, perhaps Elsa was right. Just like Elsa, we should all be excited about, and thankful for, even the smallest of miracles, too.

Elsa hosts twelve friends at a pre-Christmas party 11-30-08, at Seasons 52, Fort Lauderdale, Florida. photo: Judy Wallace, friend and Elsa's seamstress, Elsa, Bill Sheffield, friend and Elsa's florist for her 95th and 100th birthday parties.

September 2007 interview with Barbara Walters for April 2008 longevity
show entitled: "How to Live to 150 - Can You Do It?"

No Green Monster ... Or Untimely Criticism

If malice or envy were tangible and had a shape, it would be the shape of a boomerang.
Charley Reese, journalist, born 1937

To avoid criticism do nothing, say nothing, be nothing.
Elbert Hubbard, American author 1856-1915

Jealousy doesn't really have a positive vibe to it. Maybe it spurs some people to work harder if they want to have something. There are better ways to accomplish that. It was one of those "light bulb" moments when I read a concept in an Abraham-Hicks writing and Wayne Dyer's materials. It was about how actually admiring those people and things you want to be like or have, and blessing those people, can bring you the same for yourself. By creating negative thoughts about what you want by being jealous, you are telling the universe these things upset you instead of that you desire them. Instead, think positively about what you like and that sets up your subconscious to tap into the forces needed to get what you are seeking.

Joel Osteen says God cannot help you if you are negative because that does not allow the blessings in. I also can imagine that feeling sorry for yourself easily can make you miss uplifting moments like a friend's wave, a beautiful bird, or a winning lottery ticket. Your focus is stuck in "negative." A simple example is when you are looking for something like the salt, and you know you looked in a certain cabinet, yet when your spouse looks there he shows you it was right in front. Your mind was somewhere else and it plays tricks on you if you are convinced something is not there ... or convinced that there is nothing "good' in your life ... a negative self-fulfilling prophecy that you can turn around to your natural positive one with practice.

Being happy means avoiding jealousy. I have never heard Elsa utter one jealous word. She realizes people really don't want to trade their circumstances as well as their attached problems for someone else's. Elsa never was jealous when women were around her husband. She would say, "Well, why would I be jealous? If other women didn't admire him, I'd think something was wrong with him."

Elsa is always seeing the blessings in her own life and imagining what she wants next with knowing anticipation that if it is meant to be, it will. She didn't wait until she became 100 years old to feel this way, and neither should you. As for criticism, she will try to only give constructive criticism if asked, although that can be difficult for one who has had so much experience and feels she can be of help.

Timing can be everything, though. I once had a pact with a friend that she should tell me if I looked like I was starting to gain weight because I had worked it all off (again) and didn't want it to creep up once more in all my "busy-ness." (Take note: *this is not a good pact to have with a friend.*) She held up her part of the bargain and during a perfectly fun night out with a group of friends, she whispered to me she could tell I was gaining back weight. As if the look of mortification wasn't clear enough on my face, she went on that she could specifically tell my thighs were getting larger (that part everyone heard, both men and women - all eyes were on my thighs, and not in a good way). I just wanted to go home. She started "But you said …" From now on, the scale will be my only weight guide.

With Elsa, her timing is more right on. If I'm wearing a terrific outfit, but with the wrong purse, she will tell me privately and offer a better suggestion. Her favorite phrase in such a case: "That kills the outfit." Any pain is either averted or quickly disseminated. After that, further discussion is unnecessary and that combo will never be seen again.

Appreciate Food without Overindulging

After all the trouble you go to, you get about as much actual "food" out of eating an artichoke as you would from licking 30 or 40 postage stamps.
Miss Piggy

The only time to eat diet food is while you're waiting for the steak to cook.
Julia Child

My husband Mike and I have a wonderful physician that my mom and Elsa also go to. There's one piece of advice he gives we can't take, however. He says, "If it tastes good, don't eat it." Although his point may be exaggerated to get it across to us how to reduce our calories to lose weight, it hasn't pushed us to fully get the job done. The doctor also gets up at some ungodly hour to do his exercise routine for the day. We don't do that either.

We do try to take care of ourselves as best as we can manage to. It is difficult, however, for most in America to ignore the vast food choices easily found before us, and to find reasonable time to exercise as we balance work, home and family. Regardless, we truly feel our doctor cares about us and he does motivate us. He has made it clear that if we don't eat right and exercise now, we'll surely pay dearly for it later.

Having a business that serves frequent travelers and foreign seasonal visitors, I have often heard that Americans are widely recognized easily worldwide because more often than not we're the overweight ones. In the U.S., my husband read that Disney's "It's a Small World" ride favorite needed an overhaul because people are getting so heavy that the ride doesn't move along as it should. Disney attracts people worldwide, but I have a feeling that we Americans are the ones weighing the boats down. How embarrassing for us!

Elsa gets together with friends and/or family five or more times a week. This often involves food. She may play cards two times a week which is preceded with dinner and cocktails, have two or three other social or charitable luncheon or dinner events, have a women's club meeting, church, and other food-centered get-togethers. On top of that, she goes on cruises with the group from her club one or two times a year. You don't have to have gone on a cruise to have heard about the tempting food cruises are famous for.

Elsa can enjoy two of my husband's delicious hamburgers, savoring each bite (as opposed to the rest of us scarfing them down). She has found the way to manage all the temptation, though. She does eat at these socials in moderation mostly, and allows herself a cocktail or two. However, at home she'll have the other meal as cottage cheese and fruit or a diet shake. She has found her balance of really enjoying nice delicious food, including desserts, without guilt.

Elsa is an excellent cook, too. Whether she's cooking for others or just for herself, she will make it a balanced home cooked meal when not compensating for a party meal. She also likes tea – "hot, hot tea."

Elsa is known by many for her home-cooked soups, especially her nutrition-packed "New Year's Good Luck and Prosperity" German lentil soup she makes in a huge pot. She freezes it in Ziplock bags and shares it with family and neighbors. Great-granddaughter Elsa, at age five, declared "It's yummy in my tummy and has lots of vitamins." We German Americans like to add vinegar to it when served. Vinegar has been touted for healing and anti-aging benefits for centuries (for animals and people), but only scientifically proven (so far with the little research done on it) as good for digestion.

When people have suggested Elsa may want to consult a nutritionist to continue to live life so well, she has replied, "I haven't lived this long without eating nutritious foods and paying attention to any new nutrition news." I agree. Let's give credit where credit it is due!

People often want more information on Elsa's nutritional choices and any supplements she takes. She does take vitamin supplements, but just the basics (not a whole slew of pills). Elsa has received essential Vitamin D throughout her life via her enjoyment of the outdoors and seasonal trips to Florida (ultimately retiring there). Cold weather residents may want to inquire with their doctors about a D supplement in winter. It's important for many things, especially your bones. It is best received through the sunlight for most (ten minutes is enough daily for many) whereas it's relatively limited in foods (see health. usnews.com as one of many sources for more information).

When Elsa travelled to other countries with her husband Bill, they would find restaurants off the beaten path for the foods and atmosphere. They would ask questions about the spices and herbs used, and also bring home recipes. The use of herbs and spices in Elsa's cooking not only add variety, but nutrition. Researchers have proven that many herbs and spices are disease fighters, such as herbs of garlic, thyme, and rosemary, and spices such as cinnamon, clove and turmeric (curcumin).

Elsa says "I have always been interested in including nutritious foods in my diet. I knew the value of prunes, avocados, and fruits and vegetables in general. I also limit salt in my diet; I like the flavor of

"Mrs. Dash" spices and herbs, specifically the no salt original blend and the Italian medley of tomato, basil, garlic and more. I also use seasoned pepper and seven whole grain bread regularly in my diet."

Elsa believes a good breakfast is imperative. Even on a cruise, she will continue her usual regimen of a breakfast containing oatmeal (with nuts, raw sugar, and milk), prunes, coffee and orange juice (with a splash of vinegar when home). There are times she also enjoys ending her day with orange flavor, too … a slice of orange in her glass of Ketel One with three olives (in an attractive martini glass, of course). Presentation is half the enjoyment (well, maybe at least 25% of it).

And, I would hope needless to say but will say it anyway: Elsa's occasional social drink is not something she is recommending to others to start doing if they currently don't. I would be remiss, however, if I did not mention this was part of her own lifestyle. As with all so-called "vices", consider your doctor's advice and your own circumstances to balance good health and life enjoyment

There are researchers that say alcohol, limited to two drinks daily, appears to be good for you (not just wine), though (one source: study of US and England seniors over 65 by Peninsula Medical School, England, 2008). It may be because it reduces stress and inflammation, therefore helping one to avoid illnesses. Obviously, however, it's not for everyone.

Nevertheless, you may have experienced someone so entrenched in healthy choices that they had difficulty finding something to eat at your favorite restaurant. Maybe you've witnessed a spiritual guru so often in deep meditation that he is not engaged in life with others. Perhaps those choices are in their best interests and completely work for them. Regardless, many cannot argue with Elizabeth Taylor saying, "The problem with people who have no vices is that generally you can be pretty sure they're going to have some pretty annoying virtues." Even Abraham Lincoln had quoted his thoughts about people with apparently no vices, "It has been my experience that folks who have no vices have very few virtues."

From all I observe and read on this hot topic of weight control (with social drinking involved or not), it takes more than our common sense of eating less and exercising more to keep our weight in check. We need to find motivation and/or change our habits until it becomes a natural and content way of living. It takes commitment to produce the motivation and make the changes. It also takes knowing when it's ok to treat yourself a little.

For me, I did learn Elsa's appreciation of food (but unfortunately not the consistent moderation in eating it). My husband and past boyfriends all thought it a bit strange that at special celebrations at home we took pictures of the beautifully prepared meals. I never realized that was odd to appreciate the food this much. Nevertheless, presentation does make a difference whether it's sandwiches or chateaubriand.

As for weight control issues, I have heard Raquel Welch (or was it Sophia Loren? It was one of those buxom brunette beauties, although Sophia has been known to credit pasta for her figure) say she only eats for fuel and not for pleasure. That concept won't work for a lot of us. Anyway, just like the different packaging for learning to be positive, we all need to find the correct plan for us to appreciate food without overindulging.

Some of my successfully thin friends have found they need a steady stream of new diets to try to keep them motivated. Another one of my best (and consistently thin/always attractive) friends Genia is a diehard Marilu Henner fan, advocating the author's stricter plan phase of no meat, among other guidelines, with absolute success (currently concentrating on a simple breakfast, soup and salads for lunch, and a small dinner). Others, like my gorgeous (and nice!) godmother of my children, second cousin Geraldine Brehm Blair, swear by detox diet plans I may try. Motivational speaker Tony Robbins teaches you how to condition your mind so you automatically eat less and are happy about it. It helped him to lose almost forty pounds. I have succeeded previously with using a Jane Fonda diet trick: having more soup since many are low calorie and your brain gets the "full" notice more quickly than with solid foods, or I get full on bigger vegetable portions.

I look forward to finding a final long lasting solution as Elsa has that works with my lifestyle and keeps me content, motivated and satisfied. In the meantime, as I search the Internet and take diet quizzes (the ones unaffiliated with any specific products), I always find a regimented pre-packaged plan works best for me to get me back to my "normal." After that, healthy eating habits with simple exercise (walking, biking, swimming) keeps me there.

In America, however, there's constant temptation and easy access to fast fattening foods, as well as difficulty finding the time and energy to exercise in our jam-packed family and work schedules. Many find ourselves on a weight roller coaster. Until we find our own plans we can truly believe in, nothing will work indefinitely. As women like me work towards our weight goals, however, thank goodness for Delta Burke's comfortable and flattering lingerie line in the meantime (I kid you not).

Listen to Your Elders ?

Sons and daughters used to listen to their elders in Elsa's youth. Now the pendulum has swung as we reject elders' advice on many matters. We feel that we know ourselves best and we want to pronounce our independence with our choices. Neither extreme is usually optimal.

Elsa went to business school and as a teenager helped her parents start their hugely successful bakery supplies business that currently has revenues of over 40 million dollars – *wowsa* - (before that her parents ran several bakeries). Her dream was to teach physical education, however in those days you listened completely to, and abided by, the needs and demands of your parents on these matters. Elsa says she has warm and loving memories of her parents and did not hesitate to obey them (except when she secretly saw her husband-to-be after her father told her to wait over a year to date him). She worked for the family business until she married. The business is currently headed by Ernie Brehm, Jr., Elsa's nephew, who took over from his dad Ernest, Elsa's late brother.

The skills Elsa learned in her parents' bakery supplies business were easily transferable to handling the bookkeeping in her husband's roofing business and other business dealings to follow. Even her younger sister Gretchen had worked at the family business, in charge of rationing during the war, which was a very important role, too. Later Gretchen married and moved with her husband to California, eventually finding their own business success. Elsa's younger brother Ernie learned from her dad how to take charge at the business while her other brothers Hugo and Otto were off on their military commitments. Ernest was an outstanding president. Elsa is the only remaining child of her siblings, and the oldest remaining past employee.

Now Elsa has given me great advice over the years, from style to business to relationships. I often take it, however I did not always take her advice that would have been the way to go. Elsa has business experience in four distinct areas: her parents' bakery supplies business, her roofing business with her late husband Bill, a Florida motel resort she and her husband owned and operated, and real estate flipping and renting (their three R's: roofing, resort, and real estate). She has flipped condos well into her senior years and would do it again if the opportunity was right. She also has lived through all kinds of economies of this country's history.

What is wrong with me that I did not take her advice when my husband and I moved to Florida in 2000? She advised us to buy a duplex so we could rent out the other part of it for additional income as we started our business, but we had no interest in that. Then when we saw a villa home for a bargain price, why did I insist on cancelling the deal after we had put in an offer and deposit (aside from the spiritual "sign" I thought I received after reading the community newsletter on the current resident's frig that said "A severe financial penalty will be levied on the person who has been defecating in the pool; You will be discovered.")? It was so strong in my mind that if we were picking up our lives and moving from NJ to FL, that I just had to have a place by the water.

We ended up finding a more expensive place by the waterway and within walking distance to the beach, but starting up the business had cost way more than we had planned, and the financial stress was at times unbearable even though month by month we saw how the business was growing. Elsa hadn't pushed me and even if she had, I probably wouldn't have listened. How could I not heed her wisdom from her years of experience? It's that Boomer thought process of wanting what we want now and thinking we always know best ... and having less patience ... and knowing that we will work hard to try and skip steps normally needed to get where we want to be, especially since I had already hit 40 and Mike 50 years of age. It was difficult. I hate to admit it, but like other Boomers, there have been times like this that I probably would have taken the advice of an old Indian sage before our

Elsa. We think other more mysterious exotic cultures have the secrets in their elders' advice without realizing our loved ones here know secrets, too, and they know us best. We need to listen more to our "American sages", and Webster's needs to change the meaning of "sage" to include "a very wise woman" instead of only "a very wise man."

Let it Be

There is nothing that wastes the body like worry, and one who has any faith in God should be ashamed to worry about anything whatsoever.
Mahatma Ghandi

If you can't sleep, then get up and do something instead of lying there worrying. It's the worry that gets you, not the lack of sleep.
Dale Carnegie

Let it be. Those words have calmed many aching souls. Elsa has a similar philosophy: Do all you can to resolve a matter and then "just put it out of your mind" using prayer and relaxation like the yoga technique (consciously relaxing each part of your body, one section at a time) to help you rest.

A recent challenge for Elsa was with a shutter company. Hurricane Wilma ripped apart our shutters and decks at the building Elsa and our family lived in when it hit. It took over a year to get the decks redone and up to code. Then there were the debates on what kind of shutters would be up to code and also look good. Elsa was on a corner and had a bigger deck than our interior unit. She opted for the motorized kind because for most people, let alone a centenarian, moving shutters up and down manually can be labor intensive. The company took a $6,000 check deposit and later announced they were out of business. My aunt said she had a contact that will help in trying to get the money back, so while that is at work, Elsa will just put it out of her mind and let it be. I wish she had put it on a credit card so she could have disputed it, but of course hindsight is 20/20.

I have been dubbed "the emotional one" by friends and family. It seems to be my best and worst personality feature. People love it when I understand their feelings and can make them feel better or help them resolve a problem. They hate it when I am easily offended. I could blame it on "the middle child syndrome" or my lot in life as a "sensitive Pisces", but whatever the reason, I've worked on it rather than make excuses. Regardless of the "emotional" designation I was given, my mom says she is impressed with how I've always had many friends, and how I keep in touch with them as well as I do. Also, running a business has made me thicker-skinned. I have all the problems and concerns of my generation from financial worries off and on, and what the future holds for my family, to wondering how I possibly can get to all that needs to be done on my "list." I deal with it all quite well, though, if I do say so myself. Prayer, then "let it be", helps me.

The most unusual problem I had in my life was some alien visitations as a child, or certainly something very, very strange (and not sexual if you're thinking that!). To this day, I don't think anyone has believed me, even my mom who left her body when she was exhausted while doing the family laundry one day, and she's also seen at least three spirits. The limit on most of the family for thinking out of the norm on spiritual stuff is reading their daily horoscope in the newspaper (Elsa likes reading hers as well as other family members').

More than one person has told me confidentially that they have seen what they believe was an angel. One told me that an angel protected him from having a car accident. They don't want to share the information with a lot of people, though. Some day our beliefs will allow more to share these experiences in detail without fear of being judged. According to Fox News (Harris poll), 71% of Americans believe in angels (12/2008). About 6 in 10 Americans and Europeans have had some kind of psychic or paranormal experience as surveyed in the mid-80's (Haraldsson 1985).

When I lived in N.J., I had a "psychic party." It was just for fun, but my husband Mike escaped and went out with his friends, saying he hoped he wouldn't be returning to the vortex of hell spinning around our condo. We all survived and many were impressed. We just can't possibly know everything about the spiritual realm, no matter what our religion. Anyway, I stopped the visitations by praying it wouldn't happen again. I prayed that for years.

Now I can put it out of my mind and let it be.

Don't Rub It In ... Rub It Out

I heard this phrase above most recently during a sermon I saw on TV from a Grace Place church service out of Stuart, Florida, from Pastor Rick Addison (thegraceplace.com). The point was made that people need each other through thick and thin. Nevertheless, when it's thin, your uplifting support is needed, and not a commentary on how all could have been handled differently when someone is suffering from an error in judgment, or from anything else. Just like the book <u>Men are From Mars, Women are from Venus</u> (by John Gray) taught in one example, there are some times when you are not needed to try and fix a problem. Instead, you're needed just to be loving and supportive.

Elsa's actions consistently demonstrate this insight. When I am upset about something, she knows. Some would back away, thinking the upset person needs some "alone time", or "time to settle down." Elsa gives me the chance to make that decision on my own rather than assuming my needs. She just comes out with that simple yet profound (as in deeply effective) phrase, "Do you want to talk about it?" The last time she did that, I said yes and my tears flowed as I got it all out. Although the situation had not changed that upset me, tears release stress and the connection I felt from someone who cared was cathartic. And, although I know her and I know from the book called <u>Passages</u> (by Gail Sheehy) that seniors have a difficult time not sharing their views on a matter since they have so much valuable experience to share, she knew I just needed her to listen to acknowledge my feelings with the sincere and caring heart she always possesses.

The preacher's sermon mentioned above also brought to light how damaging a mean comment can be to someone and how important it is to bring people up daily as the Bible verse in Hebrews 3:13 states, "Encourage one another daily." This could be Elsa's mantra.

She takes the time to give sincere specific compliments to people she encounters on a daily basis, and I've never heard her utter a cruel word about anyone. The preacher also said a study of 10,000 depressed women found that the cause of their depression was of not regularly feeling uplifted or affirmed by anyone. Yeah, I get that we need to take responsibility to do that for ourselves, too, but part of that is keeping yourself in the company of good people that appreciate, acknowledge, and encourage you. Remember, we're not just talking about special holidays. We're talking *daily* here to make people feel as special as they are.

In the upsetting scenario I had in the disagreement I spoke of above, someone had spoken very cruelly to me after a fairly trivial difference of opinion (no, it wasn't my husband). It was obvious he was stressed or upset about something else and took it out on me. Nevertheless, that ugly talk, once said, stays with you and is hard to shake. This negativity makes a much more pronounced and long lasting impression on one's emotions than a compliment of the same magnitude brings one up. That preacher said one study concluded a compliment weighted against ugly talk of the same degree affects someone as ten times worse (yes, 10 times more potent negatively than by the amount a compliment's potency uplifts someone - worth saying again!).

Hold back on saying mean things out of anger to anyone, and especially to children that need your support to grow in confidence and love. I am there. I have two small children and I get upset and lose patience, but I stop myself before saying anything I will regret. When children do not behave, they need to know there are consequences as there are in life in general. Trying to teach them that is not always an easy task, but letting them know taking away privileges or having a "time out" is teaching them to be good and happy people by learning proper behavior is a must. It is done because you love them and care about their upbringing. They might not understand it entirely and immediately, but one day it will sink in.

Elsa stresses kindness and truth, saying "we cannot do wrong and feel right." These words and train of thought are clear in her favorite poem, entitled "Nobility", by Alice Cary. It has been a strong influence in her life since childhood. She gave a scrolled copy to everyone at her 100th birthday gala.

Houston, We Have a Problem

Don't make me get out my flying monkeys.
The Wicked Witch

Adopting children, especially internationally, can test your skills of organization, patience and emotional control in ways you never thought possible. No matter how successfully you have done the mass of paperwork, there's always one more unexpected addition, and it needs a special "apostille" from the state, and it needs to be done now … with overnight handling. That's hard, but how about meeting your children for the first time, but knowing they can't come home with you until a month later? (Recently we watched some video of our two trips, and my four year old Elsa asked why we didn't take her with us when she saw us leaving her the first time.) Then, huge hurdle #3, when it is the final trip to Russia to get them back, there's a hurricane and your flight is cancelled. Each of these scenarios required us to take action and get it resolved.

Some things cannot be handled by someone else. The paperwork was a pain, but doable. Explaining to our children (now that they know English and are old enough to understand) the story of the rules and when we could bring them home wasn't half as bad as the emotions for us waiting in-between the trips at the time. The girls really didn't absorb how dramatically life was to change for them, but we knew and we couldn't wait. As for the flight cancelled, our ever supportive and smart cookie adoption agency contact (Brenda Baker) told us to go to the airport anyway and get a flight (usually more successful than the phone in this case). She told us she even had parents flying to adopt on 9/11. We not only had the hurricane on our minds (ended up more north), but Russia had three terrorist attacks the year we went there (2004). When the Russians asked us if that made us fear travelling there, we said no. We took certain precautions for safety (and we had the remaining cash we needed strapped to our bodies under our clothes). Nothing was stopping us from completing these adoptions.

If this all didn't seem overwhelming enough amongst our excitement, I carried a big secret along with me. After giving up on having a healthy pregnancy myself, I discovered I was pregnant before our trip! Of course we kept it to ourselves because we did not know if that knowledge would affect our adoption process. Experts claim this pregnancy upon adoption story is a rare one, but we all seem to hear it a lot. I believe our mind accepts and prepares ourselves for things, like family, when we believe it is possible. I later lost the pregnancy, but something was going on there in my beliefs preparing me for our family.

The strength I needed sometimes seemed to come out of nowhere, but I knew strength and the power of love from Elsa's example. I saw her make sacrifices to keep loved ones connected, even when there was a disagreement and she knew she was right. I can share one involving a neighbor and friend when Elsa and Bill owned the Jasmin Villa Resort Motel in Pompano Beach during starting in the 1950's for about twenty years. They were on great terms and good friends with the neighbor.

During that time, Elsa was enjoying planning attractive and delicious continental breakfasts and BBQs by the pool, as well as cocktail hour with Bill playing the piano in their large apartment. Additional landscaping and trees were planted for beauty as well as so not to disturb others with the hum of those socializing. But suddenly Elsa noticed her neighbor was very cold to her. She stopped waving and didn't bother to walk over to say hello as she used to. Elsa thought this was very strange and she wanted to see what was wrong. It was something she felt she must address herself, so she marched on over and asked if something was bothering her. The neighbor said, "Elsa, we just can't believe you put up trees between our properties." Elsa replied that she thought the parties may be disruptive to them, so she assumed they would be happy to have more privacy and quiet with those trees in. Elsa's friend said, "Oh, no! We love watching out our window at those parties." So Elsa invited them to come anytime to join in, and they did. They continued to enjoy a wonderful long friendship.

Facing a problem may seem overwhelming at first, but taking it on more often than not will yield results that may surprise you. When it's your issue to solve, time is of the essence rather than worrying about it. You are stronger than you think you are. In addition, your simple and sincere communication is often the cure for misunderstandings.

Humor for Healing and Making Your Point

LOL

Abbreviation used in text messaging for "laughing out loud"

Laughter is the shortest distance between two people.
Victor Borge

A woman I did not know came up to me when Elsa turned 95. She was one of many that were in awe of Elsa's outlook, health, and attractiveness, especially for the "advanced" age of 95. The woman asked me if my late grandfather, Bill, was a good husband. I replied he was an unbelievable husband to her - romantic, hard-working, loving, a very fine pianist, humorous and would wear whatever Elsa put out for him, even if it was a salmon colored sports jacket (which he looked great in, by the way). She immediately said, "THAT is her secret! Her wonderful marriage made her this way!" Then she confidently walked away as if she had solved some great mystery of the world at least to her own satisfaction.

My grandfather Bill was called Dadeo by us grandkids. He was all those things I mentioned above and more, and though he passed long ago, I recall him with such fondness and love in my heart. I can also still see him saying something funny and Elsa trying to hold back her smile because she was trying to talk about something that needed to get done or needed attention. He helped her to not take things too seriously and to enjoy humor often. It was rare they had any big disagreements, and we never heard any firsthand.

There was one weekend our family was visiting, however, and we were touched by Dadeo's romantic gesture of picking a flower every morning to leave on the breakfast table for Elsa. On our second night, however, there must have been a disagreement. When we woke up to look for the romantic flower, there was a flower there, but it was all brown and dead. When Elsa saw it, she couldn't help but still smile as usual due to her husband's unique and creative humor, putting whatever it all was into perspective…. And hopefully averting any before-bed arguments in the future since as we all have heard countless times, you should never go to bed angry at each other.

111

My husband Mike makes me laugh daily. It works to give me that rush of serotonin just when I need it. Whether it's bedtime and he pulls his underwear up to practically his nipples and walks around in shuffling-along- in- tiny- steps like the Tim Conway's elderly character stint from "The Carol Burnette Show", or he does the Pee Wee Herman dance in the same, he knows how to crack me up (although this behavior is less effective as a sexual prelude).

I too use humor as much as appropriate. It's a method to use to sometimes diffuse stress or to mediate disagreements, most always with favorable results. Relax watching some funny movies or sitcoms now and then. That will give you some easy inspiration to try out yourself as well as laughter to release tensions. Some go as far as to say humor is an illness healer. Try it. You'll like it.

Elsa not only appreciates it, but can come out with her own humor, adding her own splash of panache. Although it happened long ago soon after she met her future husband, this story is a family classic of her quick wit to make a strong point. Being in the bakery business and later supplying goods to bakeries, Elsa's parents perhaps were ahead of their time in keeping a spotless super clean work environment. Meanwhile, Elsa's love Bill toiled away with his roofing business, in a trade where even the cleanest person likely could not scrub all the tar and grit away from the day's laboring. Elsa's parents adored Bill (he was German descent also, hardworking, successful, and entertained friends and the family playing piano). Regardless, one day Elsa's mother couldn't hold back and she said, "Elsa, you know how clean hands are so important to us and to our business. What is that dirt under Bill's fingernails?" "Mama", Elsa confidently replied, "That is not dirt. That is money."

Love and Affection

Love is not a constant topic of conversation. It's a way of being. You have to have consideration for the other party. I try to see things Elsa's way as well as my own.
Bill Hoffmann, Elsa's late husband, during a media interview on their 50 years of marriage

The way this man adores his wife through the years everyday...
the way he truly enjoys the beauty of flowers; This man is a true
romantic.
Dent DeLong, late brother-in-law of Elsa, speaking of Elsa's
husband Bill

Despite how funny my dad always thought it was that my mom brought
ice skates with her on their Lake Placid, New York winter honeymoon,
passionate love is not only reserved for the young. Nevertheless, in Elsa's
case, she has had little to no desire for another life partner since her
husband passed. She is surrounded by loving friends and never feels
uncomfortable or lonely at social gatherings. Elsa did have some steady
escorts, but she outlived them. She cherished these friendships, but did
not wish to marry.

Elsa is certainly in healthy and attractive physical form to date if
she wanted to, so I know she could make it happen for the right man.
She just hasn't needed that and has made her feelings clear on this. For
example, when I saw a man making a move on her by massaging her
shoulders as she washed a dish over the sink, she turned around and
asked if he would be kind enough to take out the garbage. (That's "senior
talk" for "Please don't do that / not interested.")

On the other hand, one of the other cents on the Walters aging
special had a younger boyfriend (only 94!). They described their dates
which consisted of meals together and bridge games. A blogger on the
ABC site comments section inquired if "bridge" is some sort of code
word for senior sex. One never knows. When I took what was considered
a "gut course" at Rutgers entitled "Sex and Pregnancy" (in the early 80's),
I actually learned quite a bit. I still am surprised we were shown a film of
a senior couple (as well as a couple with one partner being a paraplegic)
being intimate. The point, of course, was sex is enjoyed and happening
with more than just the active young college crowd.

So back to Elsa and another way of looking at the subject at hand:
She still loves classic movies and the sweet innocent romance found there,
although she reads a lot, too. Elsa is shocked and aghast at what appears
on the printed page of best sellers (raw wild sex that she often skips over),
so she has more than a clue what you all are doing out there. Regardless,
she is one fulfilled woman with her memories of a loving and near perfect

marriage. Even after her husband's death, she did not allow herself to become lonely or alienated like many in that situation complain about. Once you get it together again (even a little) after a spouse's passing, you have to reach out and get active socially again, regaining happiness and appreciation for what you had and what good lies ahead.

With Elsa, friends shared their husbands with her for dancing partners. Other male widower friends have been her escort here and there. Often it is perfectly acceptable and comfortable for her to go it alone to parties and social get-togethers, or along with other single women friends. Living with passion, love and affection is much about sex for at least parts of our lives, but there are other pleasures that fill that type of passion cup, too, as Elsa shows daily with her love, caring, and closeness to family and friends.

My husband Mike and I can attest to the fact that adopting two small children when your friends of the same age are seeing their children finish college and beyond is not a recipe for a consistently passionate and active sex life. Nevertheless, are we affectionate and appreciative of each other, as well as polite to each other? Yes. Do we have friends and family we are close to? Yes. Are we happy and feel love from each other and those we are close to? Yes. As I see from Elsa's example, that's the main question and answer to pay attention to when you do your love and affection overview. That's the lasting high.

Cleanse Yourself

Ahhh, if only I could always keep it simple and "cleanse" myself of internal toxins and stress like my grandmother does with things like a nice bath (alone) or Absolute on the rocks while socializing with good friends, along with her overall healthy eating habits. But no. Generations after Elsa's collect more toxins and stress than ever and then want to dislodge it fast and furiously (think of a certain Rolling Stone with a heroin detox blood filtering in Switzerland in 1973 ... or was it an actual transfusion like an embalming as he once said it was and later recanted? ... we may never know).

When I was nineteen, along with a friend and my mother, we volunteered as extras in a movie called "Mother's Day". We were told it was a horror movie like Hitchcock's. Later we learned it had some pretty violent icky stuff in it as three men brutalized three woman on a camping trip to the delight of the men's mother. Anyway, our small parts took all day to tape. The scene was an EST seminar (Erhard Seminars Training, popular 1971 to 1984, 60 hours intense workshop) for personal transformation and enhanced power. Perhaps the concept was exaggerated, but we were to look as if we had been in the warm room seminar for hours without bathroom breaks, becoming very uncomfortable and sweaty. I wanted to look good in "My movie debut", but they kept squirting me with water to look sweaty! They fed us donuts to keep us going. Some people snuck out because it actually was a long and boring day. The producer was freaking out because if people left, it messed up the scenes. EST is one seminar I am glad I missed if the film was anything close to the real thing. Regardless, many swore by it for 13 years until it reformed into something else.

I have been pulled into the hype on detox products. I went on an "ultimate cleansing" with a lemonade drink consisting of organic lemons, maple syrup and cayenne pepper after being inspired by success stories online. Well, I felt fine for 24 hours, but then experienced every side effect ever associated with that cleansing routine. I ended up very sick and was medicated with antibiotic to recover. The "foot detox pads" were a safer product to try for me. I still have some if anyone is interested, although my mother may stock up with my supply. She swears by them for alleviating leg cramps. Anyway, I always say "never again on 'miracle' products, but ..." Others get something out of these things, so if it floats your boat, whether it's mind over matter or not, by all means do it.

Perhaps I am somewhat bold to admit my experiences above, but others have revealed similar stories to me, too. One of the contractors we work with regularly through our business, our Brazilian friend Julio, told me about his Arizona, Indian sweat lodge (tent) experience for spiritual cleansing. He was feeling too warm to start with when he entered into the tent with a group. All were so serious and anxious to see spirits and to be spiritually transformed. All that Julio could think of was finding a cooler place to be, but he thought the ceremony shouldn't be too long. His friends wanted to share this experience with him, so he didn't want to disrupt the proceedings. Hours seemed to pass and as he lay back, he tried to sneak his nose out through the bottom of the tent for some fresher cooler air, but he wasn't too successful. Julio worried a wrong move would reveal his lack of proper group concentration and that would wreck everything for all. As time went on, he was startled to hear others excitedly pointing out that they were seeing spirits. It appeared that the sooner all saw their spirit guides, the sooner this thing would be over. Julio saw nothing. He couldn't take it anymore, but he had endured it all this far without ruining the experience for others. Julio did what he had to do. He created the performance of his life by imitating the shock and awe he witnessed by the others. It was finally finished. (Nevertheless, I would love to visit Sedona one day. I can't help it!).

Elsa, as elegant and poised as she is, has been known to say when appropriate, "Always remember the KISS method: 'Keep it Simple Stupid' (without really calling anyone stupid directly)." Many of us worry way too much about this cleansing when simple care seems to work best as Elsa has proven in her case.

Concentrate more on "keeping it simple" with less processed foods, more social enjoyment, and at least some physical activity level above "sedentary" or "couch potato." Add on your own thing like a walk, a good movie, a nap, a good read, an excursion, an orgasm (the drink, or the real thing). Actually, I didn't know about the drink until my friend Linda H. and I were out in our single days after work, probably in the late 80's. Some guys sent us over drinks called "Screaming Orgasms." The waitress said they thought we "needed them." Perhaps we looked stressed, but it didn't take long before Linda was dancing on the bar (way, way before the "Coyote Ugly" movie made it popular) as she dragged the closest man around by his tie. Memories. Good stuff.

Overcoming Hardships

Schwamm darüber
German expression for:
Swim over it; rise above your problems

Forgatabout it
"Forget about it" in urban New York City accent

I believe we are born to see things in a positive way and keep envisioning new desires that actually come about due to our optimistic views. Unfortunately, we let that thought process slip away as we learn the wrong way to think from other influences. I re-learned this natural "law of attraction" directly and indirectly through trial and error, writings by various authors such as Abraham-Hicks, and Elsa's real life example. I used to think if we just keep imagining the worst case scenario, you'd be prepared for that and happy if it came out better. That's not such a great way to live. Regardless, one of author Dale Carnegie's methods to overcome worry is to think of the worst case scenario, adding another caveat to it. He says then you realize you can survive that. After that realization, it opens your mind to action and solutions rather than wasting time worrying about a problem. Ultimately your attitude is refreshed back to positive.

Although some may claim Elsa's life looks like a story book and that's what must make her naturally optimistic, my observations and research about her life show example after example of life experiences that others would find impossible to get past and would allow to negatively impact the balance of their life experience.

Look at this overview, a partial history of Elsa's adversities overcome ...

A woman born into a family where one of her brothers died as a baby, yet the family accepted and grew and flourished ... A strict and absent father who worked so many long and odd hours , that as a little child, the daughter thought her father was her uncle because he was never around! ...Parents that put the young girl to work doing things such as scrubbing three sets of stairs regularly (employees of the business that lived upstairs felt badly for her, telling little Elsa they would try to skip every other stair to make her job a little easier) and polishing all the brass fixtures. As she became a young teen, she was told she could not be a teacher as she dreamed of, but had to take business courses and continue to help build the family business. This girl finds a man who wants to marry her who she also loves dearly, but her father tells the man to come back in a year. Then when he comes back in a year, her father says come back in six more months. When he does come back again and they marry, her desire to be a great support to her husband's business as well as a perfect wife and mother brings her to a nervous breakdown. She recovers. As their family grows, Elsa and husband Bill yearn for one more child. Sadly, the doctor tells them it is too late. (Later Elsa gets pregnant and Pamela is born.)

Don't forget the pressures and painful events endured of being family matriarch with all the trials of other families ... surviving The Great Depression, relatives struggling financially while others are wealthy, relatives suffering with alcoholism, divorce, cancer and depression, relatives suffering the loss of loved ones and miscarriages, disagreements that lead to a few distancing themselves from the family ... She withstood the worry of various generations of men in the family who went to various wars for our nation, with all not coming back the same as how they left. ... Seeing relatives pass... the loss of a husband and a son, dear daughters-in-law and son-in-law, as well as infant twin grandchildren and others.

This certainly is not a complete list of Elsa's challenges and losses. Regardless, it amazes people that Elsa has found a way to "deal with it" and discovered a way to find the best in any situation. After some prodding, she admits now that her hefty childhood chores likely would be viewed as child abuse today. Nevertheless, she says the chores taught her pride in her work, good values, and attention to detail. She also lovingly recalls her father's words after she cleaned up from her chores and put on a pretty outfit. He would say, "Being able to do such a good job on your chores, and then dress up and act so nicely at a lovely affair, is a sign of a true lady."

It can take some effort to make a potential negative thought into a positive one if you usually do not, however it makes no sense to live in anger, sadness or resentment. Elsa's way of acceptance and ability to manage the ups and downs as well as to concentrate on the good things in her life show a tremendous secret to living well and positive aging. It was a wake-up call to me to see how powerfully Elsa is entrenched with this life-enhancing thought processing when "anti-aging" expert Dr. Michael Brickey interviewed Elsa for his radio interview series in 2008. She had no immediate answer or long list of hardships to recite when he asked what her biggest challenge or disappointment was. Elsa had to think a few seconds, and then spoke of a financial loss she and her husband overcame (a significant property investment that later did not seem "on the up and up", so she "let the investment go"; later it would have proven to be a great investment, but they decided the stress of those initial questionable issues was not worth enduring at their age). Dr. Brickey said this kind of delayed and thought-out response demonstrated the type of research he had found: Those aging happily and well do not focus on the hard times and losses in their lives. In fact, to give examples of hardships overcome takes some thought on their parts. He said others without an optimistic view may have spoken of The Depression or the loss of loved ones as hardships they still focus on as if they were fresh in their minds and still haunting them to try and get through mentally and emotionally. Elsa has accepted hardships, learned from them, processed and overcome them, and moved on. This all is part of her ability to adapt to changes and to control her stress level. Elsa then comes out stronger than before. You have the capabilities to do the same.

In our instant Internet world, information is readily available to assist us through hardships. Nevertheless, that same "instantness" creates generations with little patience and that creates another set of problems. We need to work on that. Choose a loving and optimistic view for resolutions. It doesn't always feel easy or fast or natural at first, but wasting time on unhappiness is not what we're here to do. This reminds me of a "Star Wars" cartoon I once saw that said "The Force is with you. Force yourself."

First with the Oxygen Mask

You can please all the people some of the time, and some of the people all the time, but you cannot please all the people all the time.
Abraham Lincoln

Elsa has occasionally ruffled some family feathers. An example is when she insisted on some attending a family get-together when plans had to be changed by one group in order to attend ... and also the reverse – when she could not attend a family get-together because she had prior commitments. On the surface, this looks like she may be using a double standard, but not all decisions are black and white; other details complicated both of those decisions. On the other hand, Elsa is an inspiring example, however that in no way implies perfection.

Elsa weighs what she feels is most important as a whole, but in the end you need to go with what your gut tells you is the right thing to do. If you agree to something begrudgingly, perhaps that's not the right decision. If you will be unhappy with the result, your presence will probably have a negative energy that will be hard to hide from others. That will only put a damper on the result.

Keeping yourself in your zone so you can be strong and happy for others to support them is important. If you're acting like a martyr, you're bringing yourself and others down. People will want to avoid you like the plague. There's a time to vent and get direction and support, but if you're constantly complaining and whining, you are toxic to yourself and others. Elsa's positive outlook brings people up when they interact with her. We all need to make that effort.

Take care of yourself properly so you can be strong and positive and helpful to bring up those you encounter daily. If you are not making decisions to put yourself first, you are no good to others. This may seem totally counter to the thought we should take care of others, but you cannot help others if you ignore your own needs and then end up needing to get big help yourself. "Do unto others as you would have done for yourself" also implies you are taking care of yourself well as does "Love your neighbor as you love yourself." You should love and care for self. That does not mean you do not care for others, too.

Mental Exercise

Use it or lose it.
Neuroscientists at The University of Queensland have just published findings, which add more weight to the "use it or lose it" model for brain function.
Science Daily, 2-12-2008

We have heard enough that you need to exercise your brain to keep it at its best potential into your senior years. Those synapses need to be fed. Elsa doesn't do anything to force the issue. She finds ways to love exercising her brain. In her case, she is very social, so she belongs to several groups who play cards together at least a few times a month each, equating to games every week. In her alone and relaxation time, she loves the newspaper word search and she always is in the process of reading a book. At 101, she also continues to do her own banking.

It's compelling science about the aging brain. PBS and NPR have done numerous stories on this subject that are interesting and understandable for all of us laypersons. To sum it up, older brains still produce new neurons and scientists no longer believe we lose huge numbers of brain cells as we get older. Even simpler to remember, the aging brain can learn new tricks!

Just like finding physical activities you like to keep it fun, mental exercise can be fun, too. Game of chess, anyone?

Get a Hat

The right shoes can change your life.
Cinderella

Elsa's husband Bill never liked to see his wife upset. If Elsa was having a challenging day, he would tell her to go shopping and "Get a hat." In Elsa's long life, she had seen large hats replace out-of-vogue parasols in the 1930's, ornate hats to brighten up the boring utility fashion of clothes during wartime rationing, hats change in form to adapt to newly popular hairstyles over the years and hats used just for fun theme parties. So, for years this was a relatively small and delightful splurge item for her, regardless of whether it was for function with style or solely as a fashion accessory.

Boomers understand the uplifting nature of a splurge perhaps a little too much. Once we have depleted our energy and had enough stress and over-scheduling of our time, we often buy something big or take an expensive vacation to feel recharged again. It lasts until we get the bill for it all.

If we can tone down these grand plans until we are truly ready to afford them, we would be happier. Perhaps redefining our idea of a splurge would be in order. It might not be a hat, but perhaps a simple change of scenery with a local excursion, or buying something we truly can afford at this moment as a good start in that direction.

121

It is essential that one does not wait too long for a splurge. If you wait too long for a weekend trip or change-of-scenery excursion, for example, it may not be enough to recharge you. Coming back to the routine may be more like gravity re-entry than coming back refreshed.

Think ahead for timing. Plan ahead for what will leave you recharged. Don't overspend.

Pollyanna and Pixie Dust

As my husband and I awaited our notice for when it was time to make our trip to Russia to meet the girls we were adopting, I continued to immerse myself in research about Russian adoption. It was exciting to see through the eyes of those who had done it before us, and fun to pick up tidbits of Russian culture and Russian perceptions of Americans.

One observation Russians had was that when Russians came to America to college or an extended stay of some sort, they came back smiling all the time. Russians have been through a lot of transformation, and in Moscow they can get pretty much anything they want. Everyone is not wearing only gray and black anymore, but smiling is not yet a common sight in Russia. The result of all this is that Russians find that all our smiling makes us look like idiots. They have been through a lot, and smiling is just not in their "normal." It's not really an insult, just an observation from their life experience. Russians returning from America with lots of smiling are teased mercilessly. (I thought my fairly consistent smile was why I was easily identified as American in Russia, but our interpreter assured me that was not it. She saw everything about me as being American, although she couldn't define specific traits why. She did mention she wished all parents were as pleasant to work with as us, so I am pleased to report we do feel we were positive examples of "American ambassadors.")

Elsa has always felt a smile is powerful and can lift someone's spirits. Initially even I felt that's a "nice" statement, but perhaps statements like that were not all that helpful for the rest of us. When Elsa shares these thoughts about smiling, some call her a "Pollyanna" (referring to the "naïve optimist" definition rather than what the Pollyanna story taught:

the value and transformational power of cheerful optimism). Guess what? She doesn't care. It works for her and she is not changing.

Since I was writing about this, I started paying more attention to smiling. One day as I was walking to pick up our girls after school, I was smiling in anticipation of seeing them whereas they always give me a big welcome. As I turned my head towards a window, a young girl was smiling back at me. To my surprise, it actually made me feel really good and even happier. Science has shown again and again how smiling is good for us physiologically. I believed it even before I studied the latest research. I felt it and remembered that feeling because I was paying attention.

Using optimism for inspiration does not have to be boring, or perfect, or cute to the point of nausea, and allowing in some smiling and positivity is not a sign of naïveté' or lack of intelligence... in fact it is an easy way to enhance our lives physiologically. It's part of emotional intelligence. It's often a prelude to all kinds of success rather than only a result of it (published by The American Psychological Association as one source of this information). It's scientifically proven as beneficial within our American culture. If anything, a more intelligent and well-read person is one who takes advantage of this knowledge rather than pooh-poohs it. So think happy thoughts and smile, Genius! It works like magic pixie dust as one simple method to help you to "fly" over negativity.

Money

Er, der einen Penny nicht respektiert, wird einen Dollar nicht respekfieren.
He who doesn't respect a penny does not respect a dollar.
German saying, late 1800's

Do the math.
American saying, late 1900's

"Show Me the Money"
Tom's Cruise's famous line in the movie "Jerry Maguire"

Something in American culture and/or religion teaches us middle income Americans that having lots of money is evil. Let's set the record straight: Money is neutral. It can be used for good or bad purposes. The actual evil is a love of money - per scripture and common sense. Many big lottery winners can tell you what happens when you love the money. There was even a cable program on that topic that revealed how unhappy many of these individuals became when they got out of control about it. It didn't have to end that way for them and it won't with you. Get your perspective right and then you can let the guilt of success (looking for it or achieving it) end right here. There's an infinite amount of success and money for all of us if we want it and handle it properly spiritually, emotionally and with common sense. We can have material things and success without trading in our ethics or spirituality. By having more, you are not taking from someone else's possibilities. Elsa is a great example of someone who had successful business ventures and is also happy about it with no apologies, is spiritually content, and is a fine example of loving and caring for those around her as well as herself. In addition, Elsa's late brother-in-law Dent, who had been married to her sister Gretchen, then after Gretchen's passing married our dear Laurel from California, once said: "It is remarkable how Elsa has handled her money so well to live comfortably throughout a long life."

Elsa has seen many fluctuations in the economy. Perhaps seeing the difficult times is part of her success story in continuing to live well, yet still within her means. She never dreamed she would live so long. She is adamant about her belief in not spending more than you can afford and about very carefully deciding before moving your investments around. She also recommends borrowing when you do not need it in order to build up your credit history. This may not make sense to anyone unfamiliar with this concept, but I saw it happen firsthand with one of my husband's relatives. She always paid everything up immediately and in cash. One day she wanted to take out a small loan for some dental work. She had difficulty getting a loan because she had no record of paying off any previous loans. It does seem ludicrous, but that's how the system works. Build your credit rating.

Elsa's uncomplicated straight talk advice could have averted a lot of Boomer problems if we all weren't so impatient. Something big has happened, unfortunately, with the Boomer generation. We saw good years, made better salaries than our parents, then decided to live for now and get what we wanted now. Then we got easy credit without a thought, and as the cable news station talking heads say, we used our home values like ATMs. Now many Boomers need to get it together financially. Author and speaker Suzie Orman is my hero when it comes to looking for more detailed financial advice. She'll tell it like it is. Perhaps many need to downsize their home sizes. We personally had to take our children out of private school (we moved to a highly rated public school district, however, to compensate). Tough decisions.

Elsa still has some habits that used to baffle me. Now that I've seen some roller coaster economies myself, I grow in my understanding of her choices. She will buy an expensive pair of shoes that only go with a few outfits she has (and she'll keep this quality purchase in good shape to use indefinitely), but she will not buy red peppers because the price is too high that day. I've also seen her wash and reuse plastic cutlery from one picnic to use for the next, or even reuse tin foil that is bent but not soiled. In contrast, we Boomers dispose of anything disposable and used once (even though we separate our garbage for recycling), and if we misplace the scissors or the iron or our hairdryer, we end up going out to buy another. That's ridiculous in Elsa's world, and probably ridiculous to us, too, if we stop and think about it.

The Three Estimates

Caveat emptor
Latin for "let the buyer beware"

"We Show Up"
"Yes, we speak English"
Slogans seen on contractor trucks in southeast Florida

Elsa gets three estimates before making any major purchase. That's a good start. I want to add some more details I have learned. Problems could be avoided or rectified by knowing what to do ahead of time regarding unethical contractors or vendors.

Commonly and often with success, a lot of people just go with who their friend or colleague used for a home improvement or other item. Others just take the lowest price of a few estimates or Sunday circulars depending on what it is. As in many business decisions, however, the lowest price a contractor job offers should be thrown out if it is too low compared to the others. It is a sign of inexperience or desperation to price too low. The contractor could do a bad or unfinished job and disappear, or soon be out-of-business and you'll lose your deposit (and deposits vary by industry. Compare to know what is common practice for what you are buying.). At least check the Better Business bureau (call or online) before deciding on a contractor. Too many con men and people who don't know what they are doing are out there. If appropriate, check online to insure the business is licensed (and ask the contractor for current evidence of insurance) or call your city building/ licensing department. Do not be afraid to report any problems to the Better Business Bureau, The Division of Consumer Affairs, and the city building department/licensing board if that applies to the product or service. Use a charge card for the product/work if you can for additional dispute protection if needed.

When I first moved to Florida, I told my NJ friend Barb that many contractors and overall service industry people down here were not on the same scale as we were used to up north. She explained that it's not perfect there, either, as she recently had hired a painter that was not following the agreed upon schedule for job completion. I then trumped that by telling her we had been asking around to find a part-timer for our business. A new trusted friend told us, "I know a really good guy. He works for me sometimes. He usually shows up unless it's good surfing weather."

On the other side of the coin, I saw a bumper sticker in a small tourist shop near Tampa that said, "If it's so much better up north, go back."

Kleine Kinder
Small children

"What's a yute?"
Line spoken by a country courtroom judge in the movie "My Cousin Vinny"
("yute" is "youth" in a New York Flatbush/Bed-Sty urban accent)

Before I had children, it looked to me like those who had them shared some special secret. When they weren't yelling at the kids, they had this knowing smile that I also witnessed on pregnant woman and adopting friends (like my friend of the same first name, Sharon, and husband "Henny") that got "the call" ahead of us confirming their adopted child had been matched to them. While my husband and I talked about adopting, I also collected "data" from talking to friends and observing families as I attempted to identify the smile secret.

Most of my best friends I have are connected to New Jersey somehow or they at least have that Jersey strong passion, can-do attitude or ability to speak very honestly and bluntly about anything. You know the type. Sometimes people think we push too hard or are too assertive, or ask too many questions. Yet, later we get thanks for finding out we are all being overtaxed leading to a correction, or the community or condo budget is messed up and needs urgent attention, or after we remind the grocery store to stock up on a popular item for all our benefit, etc., etc.

Anyway, I knew I would get some real feedback from these women. One example is my friend Jo who easily relates to my challenges and understands my worries. I went to her when I had an unusual dream about owning a shop along the Wildwood, New Jersey boardwalk. It was an operation where clean decent looking guys could pay for a hug, kind of like a prostitution ring that only gave hugs. It was no kissing booth. The hugs were caring ones and of ample length.

What did this mean? Did I need more hugs? Was I worried about money? Did I want to comfort someone? Well, Jo figured it out for me. She said that this was a great money making idea that she could do with me and she wanted me to put it into writing before someone took the idea so we could get royalties if they did. She said guys liked hugs from large-breasted woman like us. Jo also informed me that the name of our venture could be "The HOW." It stood for "The Hugging-Only Whores." Leave it to Jo to set me straight on dream interpretation and small business ventures. I knew she would do the same on explaining the pros and cons of parenthood.

So, back to kids. What did Jo say? Currently in her 50's, she has grown children and young grandchildren that she obviously adores. Nevertheless, her response to me on how children change your world was, "They suck the life right out of you." I also saw my friend Barb manage play dates, boy scouts, pet responsibilities, class mom duties and PTA fundraisers. The balancing act appeared daunting to me. My friend Nancy told me not to feel I must have children. She said they become a worry from the day they are born until forever. My friend Lynn left her job to dedicate her work to her family, and she is always as busy if not busier than those of us working fulltime (although her house and car are consistently much cleaner and her family sees far less fast food and TV dinners than the rest of us who work outside the home). Another relative was told by an old friend that after she had children, she wondered, "Is this all there is?"

Some have guilt from not being with their children enough, and others have guilt for not contributing to family finances by working (and/or for their yearning to be with grown-ups more often). Some were mad. Some were overly stressed and some at times were very bored with their lives. These are all emotions anyone with a pulse feels now and then!

With all this added to our pros and cons list, I continued to have burning questions. Since my husband is ten years older than me, it is likely I will survive him. I asked him sincerely, "Who will be there for me when you are gone?" He said, "Elsa will." When I asked my sister Christine, a mother of two fabulous gorgeous children, how having children affects the family budget, she lied as she told me "hardly at all." When I told my friend Genia that we considered adopting two children, she shared that she and husband Michael were starting the process to adopt their second child from China. When my friend Nicole weighed in, she asked, "If we don't have children, what else are we going to do?" My husband had already raised two beautiful children from his first marriage, Michael and Jessica. He insists he told me it's a tough job, but I do not recall any of that.

What all these parents agreed on, however, was that whatever the ups and downs of child-rearing, it definitely had much more pleasure than pain, and added more love into your life than you thought you could hold. No one would give up these children for anything once they became part of the family. Their honesty on both extremes was greatly appreciated, but in the end I guess the decision was already in my mind before I started this quest for answers.

I get it now why I pushed on at Disney despite developing such swollen ankles from walking so much that my sister called them "cankles." I get it why my husband trudged on despite getting bit by a bee during check-in, bumping his head on a railing in Germany's Octoberfest beer hall as he bent over to pick up some kids' baseball cap, and also spending half the visit walking on a swollen knee. Our first-grader Blair included in her school report upon our return that she loved the pirates and princesses, but she really liked the nice people at First Aid that gave Daddy ice.

For Christmas 2008 our girls received a big dollhouse from "Santa" (of course secretly put together by Daddy for several hours the day prior, with directions obviously badly translated from another language and not extremely helpful). When we carried it upstairs, it became a bit out-of-joint. My husband Mike worked on it over an hour with sweat dripping down his forehead. He held his tongue as our youngest daughter, 5 year old Elsa, told us to call Santa's elves because "They know how to put together dollhouses and they had made this one." ... At that point, he did request to be left alone, though...

Growing up, I recall so clearly how Elsa would create such anticipation and excitement for any of us children visiting her. From princess-like bedding to special treats and fun excursions, she has always loved making my siblings, cousins and I feel so important. She still does the same for the children of all ages in the family, whether it is fun favors at a dinner celebration to allowing all the kids to take home the LCD mini-lights from flower arrangements at her 100th birthday party.

Children may have lots of video games and such to keep them occupied these days, but they still appreciate the attention Elsa offers to them of pure and uncomplicated kindnesses and forethought. She gives and receives joy from children whenever there is an opportunity to do so. At the same time, she teaches children to respect the time grown-ups need together without the children (spoiled kids are not an option; children do need and appreciate the boundaries).

Elsa's love of children is evident in many ways. One of Elsa's favorite photos is of seven great-grandchildren surrounding her at the beach on her 99th birthday. She adores it. It is blown up, framed, and hung in her kitchen.

Before my time, children made their own games, like stick-ball and kick-the-can. Then we had organized sports. Then we had jam-packed schedules for children including sports and music lessons, play dates, and tutors. Now many parents are overly involved in their children's higher education and their first jobs. Merrill Lynch even started a parents' day so parents could meet and greet with their grown children's bosses to appease the parents who kept calling with questions. Generations currently coming into the workplace need faster promotions and feedback more often than their predecessors. Employers are accommodating all this, and giving smaller, yet more frequent raises. It all seems a little over the top, but we need to understand the changes to work them out. Elsa listens. This is a trait that transcends the challenging changes like these, and a trait all generations welcome.

On a positive note that we all can agree on, it's terrific how the younger generations feel they are not only Americans, but citizens of the world (although this thought was previously proclaimed by such diverse people such as Socrates, Martin Luther King, Jr., Ronald Reagan, Black Foot Native American Shirley Kermali, Tom Paine during the Revolutionary War, John Nash from <u>A Beautiful Mind</u> by Sylvia Nasar, and most recently, Barack Obama). They have a desire to see the world and to understand other peoples without bias; they may be our first racially colorblind generations. Finally this belief/thought process has become more universally accepted.

We should also be sure to also engage these young generations in further understanding within our own multiple generations to seek common ground. What's your unique way to handle the critical questions? Whatever it is…Be confident, be prepared, and be yourself.

How many million times does one have to hear, "If you don't show you believe in yourself, how can anyone else believe in you?" It has been said that we know much more about the moon than our deep vast oceans. Let's not let the same happen when it comes to learning about other cultures. Learning about our multi-generations is just as important. It can be done at the same time as our multi-cultural knowledge expands.

Reaching out as Elsa does with all ages helps to bridge our differences through the generations she touches. It also helps the younger generations see a stunning example of positive aging that will affect their belief system in a magnificent way forever. We need to keep augmenting that connection through the generations by having children somehow connected into our lives, too.

For those of you in a family-forming stage, the best book ever about getting pregnant is <u>Taking Charge of Your Fertility</u>, by Toni Weschler. It teaches things you did not learn from school and likely won't learn from your doctor. If you are considering adoption, seek out information everywhere (websites, seminars, books, adoption magazines). Also, find others who have adopted to learn what the best route is for you and to separate fact from fiction. A lot of wrong and/or outdated information floats around online and elsewhere.

If the above options do not fit your situation, you could try getting closer to young relatives (my friend Mila loves spending time with her young nephew), or find a place to donate your time to help children in some way. I have read about children in Florida that live only a few miles from the beach, but no one has ever taken them to the beach. I am sure that is the least of the need out there, but it still pulls at the heartstrings. Think of the benefit both ways to be a part of a child's life to let them know how important they are.

For most of my life I did not have young children around me except during Sunday school where I taught well-behaved kids for relatively short periods at a time, or when I taught enthusiastic young cheerleaders their routines. Later when I occasionally had children in my life through friends and relatives visiting with me for longer amounts of time, the kids made me a little nervous (especially when the youngest ones had projectile spit up or did some other involuntary thing that made my sensitive stomach turn). Thankfully I got over that silliness and started to understand how children can enhance our lives and vice versa. Some children are more fun and loving than others, but all need our attention and love. They also need our good examples to emulate as well as our unwavering encouragement telling them they are more than capable to reach for their dreams and to attain them.

And, lastly …yeah, I now can confirm I also have that knowing secret smile, too.

Like a Ball of Twine – And Be Unique

Little by little does the trick.
Abraham Lincoln

To thine own self be true.
Polonius in Shakesphere's "Hamlet"; Whether this character was acting foolish or wise throughout the story, this most quoted line has to make one see the wisdom held by this human character … and the possibility that any foolishness on his part was the act.

I have been on both sides of the interview table. It can be quite shocking to hear the interviewers get together to compare their raw notes when getting down to select the "best" candidate for a job opening. I even saw some of this back in my sorority days when it came down to choosing who would fit best into the group. In a way, this "Miss America Process" of weeding out qualified candidates due to one quirky thing "wrong" seems so unfair, however decisions need to be made, so it does come down to that more often than not.

A good manager will try to make a team that is comprised of many profiles, from a leader, to a creative thinker, to a workhorse and detail person, etc. On top of that, a team should be picked that will work well together whether the boss is in at work or not. Often managers want to believe they have to be there for things to run smoothly. Some want to hire all people that are just like they are. Those ego views are the farthest from the truth for success. A good boss will know these things and look for the real you in an interview for her benefit as well as yours.

I have heard interviewees practically recite verbatim from the most popular interview technique and manager advice books on the market at the time. Answering so perfectly and rehearsed is a big turnoff. That's probably why some strange questions started appearing in interviews to try and get candidates to use their own brains to creatively answer questions. It even touched the entertainment world to spice up celebrity interviews. Remember Barbara Walters asking Katharine Hepburn what kind of tree she would be?

Something I answered in interviews (as an interviewee) was the example Elsa shared with me that she learned from her mother-in-law. I used it when the inevitable question came, "How do you handle a stressful workload when there seems to be too much to do?" Well, part of my answer was this lesson passed down from Elsa. It was to treat it all like unwinding a tangled ball of twine. Just start at one end. Bit by bit it all gets done. This is true whenever you feel overwhelmed by whatever is happening in your life. Just get started and know with confidence it will all get done.

It's not like I want everyone to use this. It worked well for me, but use your own family stuff! The point is, whether for a job or friendships, be your own unique self to be attractive to others no matter what their profile happens to be. At the same time, be open to people different from yourself for work teams or for friendships. I have had longtime friends with personality types all over the map (except for mean ones). My life has been much better for it. One of my best friends, Genia, was once asked by a mutual acquaintance of ours if she had a similar personality to mine since we were so close. The acquaintance laughed as he told me Genia's response was "No! Sharon and I are not alike at all!" If I didn't know her well and know that she loves me, I would have been very offended by that remark (however I laughed, too). I knew she was just proclaiming she was her own unique self. That's something I love about her.

What's your unique way to handle the critical questions? Whatever it is … Be confident, be prepared, and be yourself. You can also take home the message of the question/answer example. As Lincoln stated, "Little by little does the trick." I recall when I was a child, Elsa explained how putting things away as you finish keeps things organized, even when simply making a sandwich or applying your make-up. That often works, but a busy work and family life can cause growing messes that have to be dealt with later, too. When I have a messy desk or upset house, or messy problem or upset loved one, I handle it one bit at a time to take care of it. Before I know it, it's done and resolved.

Banish the Old Visuals – Make a Vision Decision

Whether you think you can or think you can't ... you're right.
Henry Ford

Those that we see who are living long lives don't do so without powerful intent that keeps drawing. In other words, what continues the motion forward itself is the continuing setting forth of the new intent that draws life through. In fact, intending for long life assures that you must be leading the parade; people don't start diminishing their life until they stop leading and start falling back into the ranks of the parade, trying to do what others are leading them to do.
Abraham-Hicks

According to Abraham-Hicks, people can keep themselves in great health indefinitely until they are ready to move totally back into their full non-physical self (to physical death, or to heaven as most call it). If you associate a certain age with the onslaught of illness, loneliness, despair, etc., (or you let others convince you of same) that is likely what you will experience at that age. If you feel you can look and feel great until you pass on, you'll experience that. It reminds me of a conversation author Wayne Dyer had with someone new to his neighborhood. The new neighbor said that the last place she lived was not a good place to live and she didn't like the people there. When she asked what it was like in this new area she moved to, Wayne Dyer said she'd probably find the neighborhood the same here. As you probably have deduced, his point was your environment will be what you make it. To put it another way: your thoughts are way powerful in creating your world experience!

Elsa has friends and close family of all ages. She has countless relatives and friends that have passed and others that are very ill. This is a pretty constant reality in her life due to living so long, often adding more friends to her social network, and having many peers up in their years, too. She could absorb that into her vision of what happens as you age and conclude there's nothing you can do about it. She does not do that, though. She refuses to let those experiences she frequently witnesses first hand to change her vision of what her own aging process is all about. Her firm personal vision decision is not affected by what occurs around her.

One must be careful not to let the beliefs of others, even of doctors to some extent, bring down their own personal vision of health and vital living. Some books were recommended to my mother by Elsa's friend Karin Olsen's daughter, Karin Wisnovsky, when my mom was encountering a health issue (since resolved). One of the books was by Rosie O'Donnell and her doctor, Deborah Axelrod (Bosom Buddies, Lessons and Laughter on Breast Health and Cancer). Rosie may be controversial, but in this book an excellent point was made that I feel is important to repeat here. Her doctor admitted that for a long time younger and older women were treated differently when it came to breast cancer.

Older women were assumed to not need their breasts and weren't offered all the options younger patients were. Not all older women may have all the options available, but if multiple options are available, they should all be discussed. Who knows how many older women received mastectomies instead of just as effective lumpectomies for their cancer in the past. They just assumed their doctors had all the answers, so they did not question the recommendation. Apparently we can assume things have changed at least in part because women now question their doctors more and also educate themselves about their conditions and options. The beliefs on the possibilities and the value of breasts to self image, regardless of age, have changed positively for doctors and patients.

On a simpler note, don't let others affect your beliefs saying you are too old to do certain things. If I listened to the unwritten "age" rules of our culture, my life would be much different. I wouldn't have waited until my late thirties for the right guy to marry (there were some nice guys I dated, but not the right one ... and plenty of frogs that would have resulted in a total disaster if we ended up together). I wouldn't have started my own business with my husband at 40, and I wouldn't have adopted two children at 44. I sure would have missed out on a lot of bliss and personal fulfillment. Was it sometimes difficult, questioning myself if I was doing the right thing? Sure. Nevertheless, I let myself feel that way by choice until I was ready to think positive again and know I could handle it all. I did that by building better, nicer, and more pleasant thoughts bit by bit about the choices I wanted until I was immersed in the joy of it all. I made the right choices for me regardless of my age at the time. I kept my beliefs intact about being able to accomplish and enjoy things others may not advise beyond a certain age.

If you need more science to believe how powerful thoughts are, consider renowned researcher and author Bernie Siegel, MD. He saw how certain positive traits people had affected how successful their healing was. Motivational speaker and author Tony Robbins brought the doctor even more into the mainstream by interviewing him and including what he learned in his teachings. For example, Dr. Siegel found that people with multiple personalities could change their health based on what personality they were presenting with obvious measurable results. They even changed eye color with different personalities! This makes sense of the Abraham-Hicks view on medicine, too. This view maintains that medicine does not affect everyone equally due to our individual and varied beliefs that affect our health and treatment results differently.

So many people look at Elsa and are astounded, whether in person or seeing her photo. Over 100 years old? That can't be! Driving and living independently at 101? That can't be! Looking so much younger and being so happy with her life at over 100 years old? That can't be! After all that, they are excited and eager to know her secret(s). What should they eat? What should they do? Others surmise that an easy life contributed to her joyous longevity (not true!).

Elsa has been serenaded at the grocery store deli counter by strangers she conversed with after they discovered she had recently turned 100. A minister to the elderly asked her to wait there for him a few minutes. He came back shortly with flowers he purchased from the front of the store for her.

At 101, Elsa voted early for the 2008 November elections. When the poll worker at the courthouse saw Elsa's age on her identification, she was flabbergasted. A policeman there then hugged Elsa. The poll worker took Elsa outside to the long line and announced to all there "I have an important announcement. This woman who just has cast her vote is 101." Everyone clapped, with one yelling, "She doesn't even look 80!"

If Elsa's inner beauty was not shining through to others, even with her "unexpected" health and looks for a centenarian, these happy scenarios would be unlikely. Now all of these people can log in a new inspiring vision of what a centenarian can be ... and all, including Elsa, were left with a smile and a terrific memory.

A tiny example of Elsa's influence on a child's image of a centenarian is demonstrated by my daughter Blair. Her first grade class was celebrating the 100th day of school. The teacher asked the class to write what they would be like if they were 100 years old. Blair wrote that at 100 years of age, she would be "pretty" and that she would be "going to the club with her friends." Although that's not the ideal and complete answer we're aiming for, it certainly is leaps and bounds above often typically expected answers such as "sick", "lonely in an old folks' home", "sad", or "wearing ugly orthopedic shoes with slits cut in the sides to relieve bunion pain" (I jest on that last one; orthopedic shoes have come a long way, and, I actually have the bunions in our family. My sister has said, "Sharon, your feet would be pretty attractive if you didn't have those dreadful bunions"). Some could say those answers are so "80's"; Let's get a new visual of age 100 for '08 and beyond. Elsa and others show us the possibilities (pretty and: strong, smart, loved, active, happy, etc.). Look out, second grade!

Blair's teacher, Lisa Wickers at SeaWind Elementary in Hobe Sound, Florida, shared with me some other responses she got from her class on the above assignment. Some wrote they "would still be able to eat," they would "still play on the playground," "would ride a bike" and "look cool." Mrs. Wickers said some did write they would look "wrinkly and old", but even so, they listed an activity they would still be doing. Teachers like this help kids imagine living long and thinking about how they will enjoy life then. Mrs. Wickers expressed her excitement over Elsa being so active at 101 (she has a grandmother going strong in her 90's). Mrs. Kunkel, teacher of my daughter Elsa's Kindergarten class, has shown enthusiasm to our little Elsa about Elsa's great-grandmother Elsa, too.

Additionally, those who hosted Elsa visiting the school in May 2008 (Teachers Sherra Bair and Jane McGovern, Principal Green), make considerable headway towards positive aging with children early on. If the children see someone who is aging happily with educators admiring her, the children can imagine all the more clearly happy thoughts about being older rather than fearing it or being reluctant to think about it. To observe a positive model of aging is a major first step towards making it happen for them.

Why not at least take the chance that how you think has a great deal to do with a beautiful life and how others perceive you? It certainly will not hurt to imagine yourself thriving and so engaged in life through all your years in addition to all your common sense decisions in saving and planning out your retirement. It's never too late to start changing those bad perceptions to make your own better ones. Imagine yourself lookin' and feelin' great 5, 10, 15 or more years from now. What do you envision? Do you need to banish any negative visuals and replace them with positive ones? As said so well in Abraham-Hicks Publications, "What I think and feel and what I get are always a match. And so, if I want something different than what I've been getting, I have to, somehow, generate different feelings." Your usual comfort zone is not always your friend.

Choose Love – Choose Forgiveness

"Forgiveness Therapy" and forgiveness healing easily bring up nearly three million search results from Google. Even physical healing is found by forgiving. Sometimes it takes a lot of love to forgive, but without it you are suffering unnecessarily. The other party is most likely oblivious to your anger, so who wins here? I know of instances where Elsa swallowed a huge amount of pride to allow healing in a personal family matter. She could see the bigger picture of what was the right thing to do. She knew even though it would be tough, if she made the first move to heal the situation, she would also benefit. Even a simple "This is ridiculous to continue like this. I love you and miss you. Let's agree to disagree on this sensitive situation because we both feel so strongly that we are right. It's time to move on and return to a loving relationship together". This statement does not fit all situations, but find a way to free yourself, be it in person or privately with yourself if that's the only way. You get the idea. What feels like the most loving way to resolve it?

Our Boomer generation has a lot of pride. It's especially tough, I believe, for us to step forward and broker a peace after a big disagreement. Our way is often letting some time pass and just starting to talk again to the other party as if nothing happened, or just cutting that person out of our life entirely. We need to choose love and try to be better with our forgiveness so it's not going to explode in anger inappropriately later. Trying to tuck that negativity under our pile of thoughts and feelings will only block good things from coming our way. Sometimes we don't even realize who or what has us annoyed. The first thing to do is take a step back to identify the emotional irritant, and then find a positive way to deal with it.

There is a right choice sometimes to cut ourselves off from people who continue to choose complaining and arguing as their way of communicating with us. Pray for guidance and for healing for that person. Tell them your presence only seems to serve as a way for them to feed more negativity into their lives (and into yours). That needs to change or you will have to back away for the health and happiness of all involved. Pray for guidance. Forgive. Love. Live.

On a larger scale, some hurts pass down from generation to generation unless we put a stop to it. I learned in my high school history class that German immigrants to America (first arrivals were in 1608) were spared the prejudice of other immigrants because their physical features blended in. They weren't easily identified as the Japanese were who arrived in the mid-1800's, for example. They also were the majority in several places, such as in New York and Chicago when Elsa was young, so Germans were protected due to sheer numbers.

When I asked Elsa about this, she said in her experience this wasn't entirely true. As a young school girl in Yonkers, NY, she recalls coming home and telling her mother of something derogatory that was said in school by a teacher about German Americans. Elsa said her mother was not the confrontational type at all, but in this situation she turned into a tiger protecting her cub and marched right into the school. That teacher never spoke that way again. In fact, she seemed to be particularly more pleasant after she awakened to her error in judgment.

There is documented evidence of some horrific prejudice and distrust of German-Americans in America during the World Wars. In contrast, they also held key positions in the American military during World War II. History also shows many German Americans boldly spoke out against slavery when they arrived in the 1800's and German Americans fought in wars for America including the Civil War, the World Wars and beyond (including Elsa's brothers Otto and Hugo, her sons Buddy and Gail, and Elsa's decorated Navy Seal grandson Bill, among other relatives). President Franklin D. Roosevelt (he was of Dutch descent) named several German descent Americans to important war posts during WW II, including General Dwight D. Eisenhower and Roosevelt's personal assistant Wendell Willkie.

Elsa loves America and holds no resentments from time gone by. She doesn't even recall the detail of the prejudice she encountered or the horrible ones she likely heard about at the time. Her parents instilled in her a love of America, forgiving mistakes made by the ignorant, and being proud of the right things the country has stood for and corrected for future generations.

It's a good thing to teach our children what is right, but in addition to that, it's a greater thing to teach them to forgive and let go of hate and negativity towards others. There's no other way to final peace and happiness than with forgiveness and love.

No one says it's easy, and likely many think of the great impasse between Jewish and Palestinian peoples as one difficult example. One ray of light is a very impressive camp in Maine that brings together teens of both cultures for three weeks yearly. Camp director Tim Wilson tells the teenagers that they don't have to like each other, but should try to see that each individual is a human being worthy of respect. The camp explores the possibility of a working coexistence. It's a place away from the violence where solutions can at least begin to be discussed. It's a small step, yet a brilliant start with great hope. Perfectly named, it's called Seeds of Peace (see seedsofpeace.org). From 1993 through 2007, over 4,000 delegates from four conflict regions have graduated from the program.

Whether the camp's or Elsa's philosophies are considered naïve to some or not, it is hard to argue that efforts towards love and forgiveness cannot be bringing about something better than the alternatives. The more people feel this way, the more solutions will appear.

Don't Skip the Dr.

Whenever I get my yearly mammogram reminder, it only feels like yesterday I got the last one. Although the new digital technology is more comfortable than the super squeeze technique I recall from the 1990's, a mammogram is still not in my top ten of things I want to do this month (actually I have a happy feeling I associate with one of my super squeeze mammograms. When I got one before I met my husband, the technician said I had "youthful high density breasts." When I left a phone message for my then boyfriend at the time that I was told I had youthful breasts, he called back to ask "useful for what?"). Nevertheless, my mentor Elsa keeps up with her routine appointments and investigates any symptoms out of the ordinary, so if I want to live well, I need to use my common sense and her example. Although this is a no-brainer that does not need a lot of explanation, it needed to be mentioned under its' own topic to highlight the importance of monitoring your health.

While on this subject, it is nice now and then to accompany a relative to a doctor appointment, and it is a good idea for a few people to have a list of any medications nearby relatives are taking. It came in handy one day for me when my grandmother had an unusual incident that led to a fall. The condo next door had a flood due to the ice maker hose coming loose and the owners were away for the season. Not expecting a wet dining area floor, Elsa slipped and fell. As a precaution, a few of us convinced Elsa to go the hospital. In the emergency room she began to answer the routine questions. When she repeated her birth date of October 11, 1907, the nurse looked at me as if this woman had a major concussion or delusions. When I confirmed the date, the nurse almost needed a doctor due to her disbelief.

On another hospital occasion, it was Elsa who got me to the emergency room. She found me listless with seafood poisoning when I was home alone. I had kept rationalizing away some serious and awful symptoms. Also, I was sleeping so much that I did not realize how sick and in pain I was whenever I moved, but Elsa could see immediately this was serious and she took fast action. I refused the ambulance idea because in my weakened state, I selfishly cared about my ego (let me slide on that one; I was really out of it). I didn't want to be on view to all the condo dwellers in our 181 unit complex being carried out on a gurney, with emergency vehicle lights flashing, etc.. Elsa understood and had a condo associate bring the emergency wheelchair from the office to us within minutes. She got me to her nearby car and drove me to the emergency room quickly and calmly.

Our physician had insisted my husband start exercising for health, so Mike started taking 20 to 30 minute walks four or more evenings a week. I was especially concerned about the liver profile results on Mike's blood test. My friend Lynn had told me of someone's success in correcting that issue with an herbal supplement called Milk Thistle. My research indicated it would be safe for Mike to try. His next blood test was completely normal. It could be due to anything, but these two new habits certainly could have helped. They were easy and as far we're concerned, beneficial enough to continue. Keep the options open on health issues, but research and talk to your doctor, too. Modern culture brings new stresses to balance, however we are so fortunate to have research available at our fingertips, readily available highly trained doctors, and availability of any needed supplements so easily within our reach.

There are times I wake up feeling like I have a bad cold and anticipate I'll be going to the doctor soon as it worsens into something else. In the past, I have had sinus and ear issues that quickly evolved from a cold and always seemed to need a doctor's intervention to clear up. If it gets to that, I won't hesitate to make an appointment. Regardless, I find now when a day comes that I wake up feeling like I have a bad cold, I often can feel 95% better just by having a good breakfast, a nice hot shower followed by a quick cold splash of water, and a positive attitude. Later I can't believe I thought I was ill enough to spend the day in bed.

Every year, it seems, more researchers and scientists are getting closer to accepting what many already have realized the world over: the mind-body connection is imperative to be aware of to heal and care for self. In fact, the only time I have seen Elsa seem "down" without obvious reason is when someone (a doctor or a loved one) tells her to "take it easy" and stay home a few days (out of concern and love, of course). Yeah, she needs to keep up with her rest, but she knows herself and knows when she is ready for more activities. Elsa is energized by getting out and about and being with people. Listen to your doctor, but also know yourself and what you can do and feel to be strong, energetic, and healthy. If you're feeling down, start doing something different.

Einstein had defined insanity as "doing the same thing over and over again and expecting different results." Others say that's more about neurosis then insanity. Nevertheless, the point is so obvious when you read it, but sometimes not so obvious in reality until you analyze why you're unhappy about something. Do you need to do more, do less, make new friends, cut out some negative friends, get outside, get more rest, read more, call or write to someone, volunteer somewhere, or find people, movies, and books that make you laugh more? Make that small effort. Make the change to get different results as needed to positively affect your emotional and physical health.

Don't forget about helping others by supporting them with their health, recovery and outlook, too. There was a time I went to the radiation oncologist doctor with my mother. She had a small piece of cancer removed successfully from her breast. The doctor said I could come right into the exam room, so I did and found a corner seat there. The doctor was younger than me, but of course very professional, competent and patient to answer questions. As he began the exam, my view was of his back. I heard him ask my mom Joan, "How does that feel?" My mom replied "That feels gooood." I almost died. To this day, my mom insists he was pushing on her back at that time, but I dunno.

Attitude of Gratitude?

When I analyze Elsa's insights of success, there is something there that I initially identified as an "attitude of gratitude" like Joel Osteen speaks about. Here is a woman who has travelled the world, had a wonderful marriage, and has loving family and friends around her daily. You may conclude that she's seen it all and had it all (been there/done that), so feeling a sense of contentment at over 100 years old now may be difficult, or boring, or even feeling more like a letdown. On the contrary, Elsa notices and admires so much that others miss. She notices a friend's new pretty pin and tells her so. She notices a new plant outside her condo building or values a new paint job that others don't notice at first. It gives her pleasure to see and acknowledge these attractive things and improvements.

As I learned from an Abraham-Hicks teaching, the correct word may actually be appreciation. The distinction is not evident in Webster's, however the lesson is significant. Gratitude may be viewed as, "Whew! I am glad I was not involved in that car accident I just passed." Appreciation is more like, "I am so blessed to be driving this safe and attractive car." Whether this semantics distinction works for you or not, the point is to be happy about things for what they are, and not because you are thankful you are better off than someone else. That differentiation is profound in how it magnifies your positive thinking power.

Listen to yourself. Are you anxious to whine and complain to whoever will hear you out? I recently gave a friend a birthday card that said we're getting to the age where we blurt out our aches to strangers as it showed a shoe salesman listening to bunion complaints. It was a joke, of course. We aim never to find ourselves doing that. Stop yourself from being so negative before people start disappearing to escape your negativity. Don't be a "Debbie Downer" like portrayed on "Saturday Night Live" (played by Rachel Dratch). Her complaining is so ridiculous that the actors can barely hold a straight face during these skits. It's so funny because some people actually behave similarly to that! Don't be one of them. Appreciate your life instead of searching for the negative.

An easy example I use for myself when I want to feel appreciation is thinking of how much I love my family. I envision seeing them after my day of work and commuting, looking into their eyes, and giving each a big hug and kiss as we begin a pleasant and fun weekend together. I am not comparing to another family or my single life prior to having a family. I am just appreciating what is, and it's all good. Consciously appreciating your world is the right recipe to benefit your level of happiness.

Beauty Inside and Out

First question you have will be answered first: Elsa told Barbara Walters that she had a facelift for her 50th wedding anniversary at age 68. Her husband wanted to get her something extra special and he asked if she wanted to take a cruise or perhaps get a nice piece of jewelry. Elsa said she wanted a facelift and her husband Bill said "That's a good idea." Some months later he told the surgeon "You have given me my bride back!" People say a facelift only lasts ten years, but that's all she has had in the cosmetic surgery category.

Elsa loves many Estee cosmetics and their perfumes, and occasionally splurges on one of their special moisturizers. When there was so much excitement in the celebration of her 100th birthday, I wrote to a few places that represent products Elsa loves. I thought it would be of interest to them and they may want to see her on the Barbara Walters special. A very lovely Estee Lauder Company representative not only responded to me, but spoke to Elsa and genuinely shared in the enthusiasm of Elsa's inspiring example. They even sent her a gift. This is a true first rate world class organization and I admire them more than words can say (and I, too, use their Lucidity make-up and one of their perfumes daily). In comparison, another company replied with something like, "Congratulations on your grandmother's 100th, but we only hire models that are professionals." What the heck kind of jaded response was that? Nobody asked for anything. We thought they may be interested, or even honored, to know this wonderful beautiful woman has used their skin lotion product for years.

Elsa watches her weight and stress as outlined elsewhere in this book. She keeps her nails manicured and neat. Caring for her teeth and gums not only is good for her health, but adds to her lovely smile. Elsa's hairstyle is modern, yet age appropriate and flattering. She also believes as her husband used to say, "A good rest is like money in the bank." Getting proper rest certainly contributes to looking well.

I gotta believe that a lot of Elsa's beauty has to do with her positive attitude, too. I once had a co-worker that I thought looked like a model. As I got to know her, she was always spewing negativity and foul language. Later I did not see her as physically beautiful anymore. Elsa's charming personality makes her attractive beyond physical traits. Her friend Leatrice Messer told me, "Elsa is one of the loveliest people I have ever met." That's huge.

Keepin' the Faith

Erst Mistus, dann Christus.
German expression:
First fertilizer, then prayer.

Faith is of paramount importance, but Elsa doesn't believe you say a prayer and just sit there waiting for something to happen. Nevertheless, contrary to what many think, "God helps those who help themselves" is not a verse from the Bible, but a quote from Benjamin Franklin. The Bible teaches to have faith in God and not earthly answers to challenges. Interpretations may vary on the Bible's overall message on this topic, but putting it all together with prayer and action you feel appropriate works for Elsa per years of positive outcomes. When totally unsure of what to do, doing something nice for another person is a method to show you the way and find healing and direction for yourself as I have also observed in Elsa's example.

My second cousin Geraldine (niece of Elsa) gave me a secret tip she has that has helped me when stressed, and I know if it helps you, too, she will be pleased I shared it. Next to her computer she has a sign that says: "Be still and know that I am God." I added another notation to that in my workspace that I observed somewhere (author unknown) that said, "Good Morning. This is God. I will be taking care of your problems today. I do not need your help. Have a good day. Love, God." Again, have faith, but if you feel you should make a decision or take an action to improve your situation … pray on it and do it.

I once had a friend who took me to a prayer group he belonged to. People there spoke in tongues and felt they could heal people. When I researched the group, I found due to some of their beliefs, they were considered a cult. "Cult" has a negative, almost devilish vibe to it for most, but some cults are really benign while others are obviously dangerous. It seems there's a lot of misinformation on the definition. Anyway, the thing that really turned me off about this sincere and nice group of people was not so much the cult designation but a woman there who told me her story. She wanted to totally rely on God and test herself that she did. She travelled cross country by hitchhiking. She had little money. She credits God for keeping her safe and bringing her back. I say this chick acted like an imbecile. Instead of testing herself,

146

I felt she was testing God which one should never do. God gave us a brain to make decisions. We should use it.

I know there are long-living people who have no faith. Others may say they must at least believe in love, in beauty, in inspiration – and these are arms of God. Nevertheless, I often notice that those who insist there is no deity or higher love or purpose of faith, have a certain gray and weathered look about them. I attribute that to the extra struggling they endure in life because they lack the recognition of a higher power for assistance, guidance, and unconditional love. They lack the glow in their eyes and skin and the energy in their step that others have from knowing this greater love.

Put in another context for believers, if you are in the majority that believes we are made in God's image, you are doing a disservice to God if you do not take care of yourself. You should live joyfully as you would want of your own children. God wouldn't make you in his image and be the Father to us all without wanting the best for us.

I love it when Joel Osteen preaches. He emphasizes that even when things seem impossible to get through or recover from, thankfully we do not have to count on an earthly solution for a way out. We have the *supernatural* strength of our Father to rely on for miracles, strength, and recovery. Sometimes when I have a problem and I need a change of mood, just listening to Joel Osteen or Joyce Meyer on television (or reading books by Norman Vincent Peale, Deepak Chopra, Wayne Dyer or Abraham-Hicks) puts me in a place that helps me find an answer to my dilemma. Their direction inspires me and gives me better focus and trust in my faith.

I acknowledge I need luminaries to help me understand the Bible and our inner guidance system. Some say the Bible has seven layers of understanding to be uncovered; others point out that all the translations the Bible has been through may have changed some words too much from their original meaning. It is the greatest book ever written, but you can and should allow others you trust to help you understand the message and learn how to listen within. One only needs to look at Bruce Wilkinson's little (but fascinating) book <u>Secrets of the Vine</u> to see how a seemingly simple Bible verse has so much more to it in meaning than your could guess (unless you're very wise and an experienced grape grower!).

147

I know Elsa could not be the enlightening example of positive aging and living without the faith she holds dear to her heart. Tap into yours to create your own unfolding and fulfilling life experience. She loves her church and attends regularly. If she cannot attend, she watches other services on television. Prayer guides and comforts Elsa daily.

As for a final note on faith, remember the importance of faith for ups and downs, and in-between. Don't lose your way and suffer only to come back for a rescue. Any day is a good day to revive or initiate your faith. Don't wait until you are sick or suffering or near life's end. Benefit from the joy now.

Family

Happiness is having a large, loving, caring close-knit family … in another city.
George Burns

To put the world right in order, we must first put the nation in order; to put the nation in order, we must first put the family in order; to put the family in order, we must first cultivate our personal life; we must first set our hearts right.
Confucius

We tend to be harder on our family members than others. We expect more from them and we know even if they get mad at us, they'll still be our relative and they'll love us (we hope). Regardless, it still shocks me to see how family members argue with each other in public. I can only imagine how heated it must get at home. It takes control, respect and more focus on love to correct this ugliness. Count to ten first if you must before you yell or say anything hurtful.

To the other extreme, Elsa is responsible for more family get-togethers of extended family than anyone I know. These get-togethers are some of my fondest memories over the years, and ones I still look forward to. She knows the value of keeping in touch despite the way we all end up spread all over America. She mediates where needed and aids in healing where it is welcomed. If a family matter is out of her league to deal with, she relies on her faith to guide her if she should step back or not.

As I age, I have become more family oriented, even before we adopted our girls in 2004. There is a special kind of comfort, love and joy in keeping contact with relatives, even when at first the effort may seem like too much to do. At the least, I try to send out occasional family updates with photos. We attend family events outside of town when business scheduling, school activities and finances permit, and consistently attend local get-togethers. Our door is always open for loved ones to visit. We remember birthdays and respond when people remember ours. Birthdays and holidays are a good reminder to acknowledge loved ones so they know you care. Engage in an effort to make (and keep up) uplifting contact with loved ones near and far.

Passion-People-Profit

When one speaks with Elsa about her life, she explains with a sparkle in her eyes how blessed she has been. Her parents taught her about business, and about family. Her father's example of starting as an apprentice until living his American dream with his wife's assistance showed Elsa what she could do with persistence. He taught her the saying in German that meant "swim over it" to overcome disappointments. Her parents also taught her about teamwork in a marriage and Elsa has always said your spouse comes first, even before your children. Your spouse will be with you after your children leave. He is your partner.

Elsa's mother's first job in America was set up by a relative to be the house assistant to a prominent family in Chicago. It was from that experience Elsa's mother taught her about the best ways to manage a home and family, as well as about quality and fine things. Since Elsa started on the family business payroll as a young girl, she had significant savings to bring to her marriage. Her husband-to-be was ten years her senior and already established in his roofing business. So, with Elsa's experience working at a young age as well as her experience caring for her younger siblings, her lessons learned from her mother, as well as her savings, Elsa appeared to be very mature and well-prepared at age eighteen to marry her business owner husband Bill in June of 1926.

Elsa's husband supported her in whatever ventures she had a passion for that was within their means. She refurbished and sold a diner, a bakery and apartment buildings in New York, for example. During The Depression, they had planned to buy some real estate and got their money out for it right before the banks crashed. People thought Elsa and husband Bill knew something was coming and were especially smart, but they really ended up being quite lucky with the timing of that move. They had an apartment building at the time. With their own funds and a program from the government, Elsa decided on the idea to make the apartments smaller so more people could afford them and so that they could fill them. It helped others and at the same time made the investment solid. One family could not pay for a year, but then they did pay up all their rent. Trust is one thing Elsa says has greatly changed in today's business dealings.

Elsa has always loved to travel. When she traveled with her husband Bill, they noticed all over the world that people travelling often looked bored and not enjoying trips they spent their hard earned dollars on. They dreamed of opening a place for vacationers that was different in one of their favorite getaway areas, the Adirondacks.

As noted earlier, with Bill suffering with terrible bronchitis each winter, the dream moved to south Florida where they purchased a small apartment complex and grew it into a beautiful motel resort. They made money on these and other ventures, however this was not a huge mass of income. The business was a means to make some money and to share with others how to have a memorable and joyous vacation, perpetuating Elsa's ongoing passion to make others happy which feeds her own happiness. They opened the resort in the 1950's seasonally, owning and operating it for about 20 years. Details of the many excursions and social get-togethers Elsa planned for her guests ranged from frog gigging to horse races to designer label shopping trips. Elsa and Bill ran it like a house party with pool and cocktail parties included. People from the United States and Canada came yearly to experience this special place.

Elsa is considered a pioneer in Pompano Beach because those who opened motels in the 1950's brought the area from just agriculture to tourism and successful growth. Elsa did benefit financially from selling the resort and holding the mortgage. The payments have long stopped, but she enjoyed having them for many years. Her passion and desire to lift people's spirits through the resort business ultimately brought her this financial comfort and profit.

When Elsa speaks, you see how optimism is such a big part of her life. Some may think that is because she's had an easy life, but as I record more and more of her life history, I see more and more tough circumstances she has endured. These are things that break other people down, yet helped her to be strengthened. She treats these things as a lesson. The strength she gains Elsa sees as a blessing. Her optimism drives her and is a huge part of her happiness and successes.

Elsa is out and about virtually every day for card playing, errands, social and charitable events, and church. One of her missions still is to make someone happy even in a small way, everyday (and she does!).

Being with Barbara Walters – Elsa on ABC Aging Special

Anything we thought was new and interesting about Barbara she admitted herself in her 2008 Audition book release, like the small, yet new revelation that part of her physical attractiveness involves the use of lush false eyelashes. She also is very tiny which may not come across to all television viewers. Gossip columnist Liz Smith made it common knowledge that the very accomplished anti-ageism author, Dr. Robert Butler, who appeared on the same show, was actually Barbara's boyfriend. And Barbara made it clear in her book that this show on aging was a favorite of hers to do and she was impressed with the centenarians she interviewed.

The interview filming actually took place in September 2007 for the April 2008 show entitled, "Live to 150 – Can You Do It?" After Elsa was interviewed, ABC wanted to film her birthday gala in October. At first Elsa thought of her guests and that the filming may intrude on the party. After speaking with family, she agreed it would be fun for all, and ABC agreed to be as unobtrusive as possible. They did a first class job. It was fun and exciting, too. So, after hours of filming in New York during interviews, horse carriage rides and fancy meals, this filming in south Florida lasted at least four hours more. Of course only highlights were on the show. It certainly shows how much work goes into the show only to have hours of the filming phased out for the final piece. Nevertheless, the clip shown of Elsa excitedly proclaiming "I did it! I did it!" (made it to 100!) with her fist up in the air at her party as all sang to her was worth every second of filming (If she wasn't Caucasian, smiling, and 100, her fierce enthusiasm could have been mistaken for a Black Panther!). We saw birthday party clips of her again and again as part of the show's promotion on commercials and morning talk shows, and still found on the ABC website. Very cool.

Barbara gets plenty of kudos for making the centenarians who appeared on the show feel welcome, comfortable and respected. The centenarians were advised that Barbara does not come out to greet her guests prior to the shows she does, but she did come out to meet them and perhaps calm any jitters of the five centenarians she would soon be interviewing. Pictures were taken by travel companions and ABC later sent on a photo for each guest with Barbara, too. And, contrary to Barbara's interviewing history of bringing people to an emotional cry, that didn't happen here.

Hold on to the Fun of Your Youth for as Long as You Can

I will do as much as I can for as long as I can.
Elsa Brehm Hoffmann at age 101

...a good and wholesome thing is a little harmless fun in this world; it tones a body up and keeps him human and prevents him from souring.
Mark Twain

A good friend will come and bail you out of jail. A great friend will be sitting next to you saying, "Wow... That was fun!"
Author unknown

Elsa recalls the fun of family get-togethers, singing and picnics as a child. The family would attend business conventions where she enjoyed dancing and quality family time, too. Elsa must have known her married life would be fabulously fun, also. It started with an Adirondacks honeymoon that lasted over a month! Since Bill knew people there played practical jokes on newlyweds (so Ashton Kutcher is not the first to start the flurry of people "getting punked!"), he told people that Elsa was one of his sisters. Later, some of Bill's brothers joined them to play in the great outdoors (Bill was one of ten children). All of this may seem unusual to us now, but it was fun for them!

As I went through hundreds of photos of Elsa's adventures over the years, there were a few of what looked like a camping trip. After Elsa absorbed them, she recalled she and Bill had hired a southern Florida park official to take them on a Florida Keys camping excursion. I thought the photo of her holding a shotgun was the surprise in this adventure, but Elsa remembers something else. She said she recalls how when their guide set up camp for the night, there was only one small tent. Elsa slept in-between her husband and the guide! She thought it a bit odd, but went with the flow and enjoyed the trip.

Elsa is elegant, intelligent, sociable and approachable, but another trait she has is being fun. Even when I was a child and we would go with her to Playland in Rye, New York, she was the coolest grandmother because she would ride the big kid "Derby Ride" that I wasn't tall enough to go on. It was like a grown-up carousel that to me seemed to go as fast as lightning, mostly with teenagers riding it. They all looked so hip as they leaned forward, with feet in the stirrups, to get the feel of riding in a horse race. Elsa also was with us when our family went to Disney World soon after it opened in the early 1970's (of course!) and to NYC shows over the years. The Sheraton in Fort Lauderdale was always a special treat on our family vacations in Florida with Elsa and Bill and extended Florida family. There was an ice show that was always a thrill.

Elsa loves theme parties for extra fun. At one of her most fabulous parties ever at her Rye home, she had the theme "Derby Day at Hoffmann Downs." A block of ice hundreds of pounds heavy was set in the front yard and carved into a derby horse masterpiece by an artist. It actually stopped traffic.

She attended to every detail of her fabulous 100th birthday party. On a smaller scale, Elsa is a participant in a party host rotation schedule with a cruise group that holds monthly get-togethers. When family gathers to eat together, she is sure to provide a special centerpiece or thoughtful pretty favors. At 100 years of age, Elsa was serenaded by an Elvis impersonator at a friend's terrific Key West themed party with frothy drinks and live exotic tropical birds. Now that's right up her alley for a great time!

Elsa's 101st birthday was celebrated with local and visiting relatives. One group met at the location of her 100th birthday for a beautiful meal. Another get-together was brunch at the famous Pier 66 rotating 17th floor restaurant in Fort Lauderdale. Elsa recalled past memories of cocktails, sunsets, and celebrations at this unique and elegant tower. The water views are fantastic. Elsa was serenaded by the entertainment with several songs. These choices for celebrating were both meaningful and very special to share with family. In addition, right after her birthday weekend with family members, Elsa and daughter Joan took a Caribbean cruise with a group of friends. These wonderful friends splurged on champagne birthday celebrations for their dear friend Elsa. The birthday girl was overjoyed with these surprise parties.

Elsa's joi de vivre and mission to be kind to others, among other things, always has kept the fun in her life. People love Elsa and respond to her. She has earned proclamations from the towns of Deerfield Beach, FL and Hillsboro Beach, FL. At age 101, Elsa was named "Grande Dame" of the historic and popular Pompano Beach Holiday Boat Parade. Birthday greetings to her have hailed from a governor, presidents and Neil Armstrong.

Fun is definitely present in the greetings and honors she has received for positive aging and living. At one point Elsa was getting embarrassed by the attention. Nevertheless, I (along with other family and friends), convinced her that her inspiring example was so helpful to others and she should just enjoy the fun of it all. Elsa then agreed to let it all ride, truly enjoying the fact she is motivating others to live more fully every day.

I usually carry a press sheet about Elsa because we never know when she will become the center of attention when a group of us family are out together. It's helpful to the reporters who are stunned that Elsa is a centenarian and want a story about her, and it keeps the positive living message spreading. Then our family can go ahead and be together, and also not disrupt others' fun with too much fuss going on.

Elsa also knows when to back out of something she has tried, but ends up to be more effort and less fun than she bargained for. During her senior years, she thought she would take up French. Despite her base of knowing two languages already, the lessons did not go as smoothly as she had wished. She decided to let the lessons go since she said, "I have done fine this far without it." This was a good decision with balanced reasoning. It also reminds me of how as a child, we can only concentrate on one thing at a time, then later we multi-task.

I've heard that as the years pass, it's not a lack of intelligence that makes some learning more difficult (npr.org, 10/30/08, Lustig Lab, Gazzaley Lab). A big factor is the fact we are so very aware of our environment, and also flooded with past memories that relate to what we are looking at now. Said another way, we have so many thoughts at once while simultaneously observing other things occurring around us now. It can take our attention away from fully focusing on the learning of something new as quickly as we used to. That can be looked at as having a big challenge of many distractions as we age. Or, we can look at it as having helpful and beautiful memories, awareness of surroundings and others' feelings, all equating to the wisdom that comes with age. It doesn't take a rocket scientist to guess which conclusion Elsa naturally chooses! And, by the way, although the researchers confirmed adults in their twenties could multi-task well, seniors excelled in telling more interesting stories and knowing more vocabulary than the younger generations

As for the topic of fun in my Florida Boomer life, I must again defer to a Disney example. I try to remember that when our family goes to Disney now and it's all supposed to be fun. Do I really feel like waiting in line to ride The Magic Carpet, or should I sit in the shade with all our stuff and rest? Sometimes it's a tough call to pay attention to balancing the possibility of heat stroke over the thrilling looks of excitement on our girls' faces. Thankfully my self-described non-Disney fan husband never has any qualms about waiting in line over 45 minutes for rides I feel are too similar to county fair rides (not worthy to wait for in Disney with all the other better options available there). Regardless, nothing is much more fun than watching my husband go up and down on the Dumbo ride with his straight face and our young girls shrieking in delight next to him. I know he especially loves it when I film him. Nevertheless, even though he's such a good sport, I still refuse to let him bring softballs into It's A Small World.

Go Your Own Way - Just Do It

Live Long and Prosper.
Vulcan salute/blessing from the "Star Trek" series and movies; Leonard Nimoy developed it based on a Jewish Orthodox "Priestly Blessing" made with a similar gesture he saw as a child that represented "Almightly (God)." The original words used on the show were "Peace and Long Life" which has both Hebrew and Arabic origin. One resource for more on this topic is Nimoy's book I Am Not Spock.

Make up your mind that nothing is more important than how I feel now, because now is everything. Now is the whole enchilada. Now is the power of me. Now, now, now, now, now... You might as well start somewhere, and it might as well be now. Why not start improving your life now, now, now?
Abraham-Hicks

Find your inspiration as needed until you are the inspiration; repeat as necessary. Only small beginning steps are necessary. Colin Powell is not going to show up at your doorstep with his satellite photos to try and convince you to do something. You won't even get a visit from Ross Perot with his charts and graphs. I have found inspiration from many diverse sources, from my grandmother, to spiritual guru Marianne Williamson (specifically her book <u>A Return to Love</u> as a start), positive thinker and author, the late Dr. Norman Vincent Peale, and also from motivational speaker Tony Robbins with his emphasis on goal setting and making decisions and actions towards those goals. As elementary as it seems, it is imperative to write down your goals to identify and to program them clearly in your mind. Get psyched envisioning them with photos you cut out of what you want. Go to the library, the bookstore, the Internet, an inspiring senior, mentor or spiritual guide … just go. If you're looking for uplifting friends, join groups with similar interests to yours. Perhaps join any number of groups at your religious institution, from Bible study to volunteer work. Follow a passion you have. If one thing doesn't work for you as motivation, try another. We're all not clones of each other. Different inspiration may vary by individual.

You cannot rely on someone else to change your situation for you, but you may need someone as above to get you motivated to get yourself together (an author through their books, a relative, an old or new friend). Elsa speaks of her husband as the one who taught her she could do anything. He believed in her and encouraged her to use her creativity and business acumen for life enjoyment as well as profit. Her confidence and passion grew with each project or business venture, and she learned from any challenges to make it better the next time. Elsa considered hardships as lessons that taught her valuable information. Her husband Bill kept her motivated by sincerely admiring her daily, and she still surrounds herself with uplifting people. She returns the favor by letting those friends and family members know daily how she values and appreciates them, too.

Do not complain if you are not making some effort to live a better life. Don't fear taking steps towards something better, either (fear it has been said is an opposite of love – gear your thoughts back to love). Living with unfounded fear is like running from zombies and still feeling fearful, when we all know zombies can't run (plus they don't exist)! Keep things in proper perspective as Elsa does so successfully.

The "You've Got the Power" Song & Dance – Your Own Zone

Intelligence is the ability to adapt to change.
Stephen Hawking, born 1942, British theoretical physicist

Imagination is more important than knowledge.
Albert Einstein

To accomplish great things, we must not only act, but also dream; not only plan, but also believe.
Anatole France, 1844-1924, French Writer and Nobel Prize winner for literature 1921

The path of least resistance and least trouble is a mental rut already made. It requires troublesome work to undertake the alternation of old beliefs. Self-conceit often regards it as a sign of

157

weakness to admit that a belief to which we have once committed ourselves is wrong. We get so identified with an idea that it is literally a "pet" notion and we rise to its defense and stop our eyes and ears to anything different.
John Dewey, Educator and Writer, 1859-1952

Become a possibilitarian. No matter how dark things seem to be or actually are, raise your sights and see possibilities–always see them, for they are always there.
Normal Vincent Peale

Celebrate what you want to see more of.
Thomas J. Peters, American Author on business, born 1942

A funky "You've Got the Power" song is popular in our immediate family because as our younger daughter was potty training, her training pants brand box included a music toy/button that she could push for this song every time she used the toilet successfully. We danced and sang with every success. We still use it for a song of motivation and victory as our girls aspire to and attain more and more positive goals.

Elsa's "personal song" is Frank Sinatra's "I Did it My Way." She is acutely aware that all the decisions she makes in her life are not uniformly supported by loved ones, yet she has the confidence to do what she feels is right and accept her decisions. She does not make knee jerk decisions and she does listen to others' opinions to keep an open mind. Many examples have been discussed in this book. I have seen her reverse her thought process on occasion when others weigh in on a topic, from financial to medical decisions and from the value of the Internet to my husband's and my decision to adopt two children. Age hasn't hardened her into myopic thinking that happens to others based on years of life experience and acquired set in stone belief systems. An open mind is definitely a youthful insight she retains and is a secret to her zone of a happy, fulfilling life.

Open your mind. It is time for you to keep making your own zone better and better. You've got the power.

A final note of appreciation
Thank you to those who share the positive living and positive aging philosophy… and to those sincerely trying to transform their lives to do so (you will get there!). Your examples serve as a great gift to others of all ages. Keep loving and keep inspiring. Live the joy.

Author Information

Sharon Textor-Black embodies a lifelong interest in writing and of seeking the best philosophies to live by. These two passions collided as her grandmother Elsa Brehm Hoffmann, whom Sharon is very close to, became a national celebrity at age 100. All who meet, or even just hear about stunning and active Elsa, want to know as much as they can about her positive aging and positive living philosophies.

Sharon soon found herself immersed in writing copy about Elsa as her 100th birthday approached in 2007. It started with various local print media and a centenarian website. Then requests came in directly from ABC. Sharon even arranged for Elsa to speak to a very enthusiastic elementary school audience of youngsters. Elsa was interviewed by Barbara Walters on the blockbuster April 2008 longevity special. Dr. Michael Brickey interviewed Elsa on his podcast (agelesslifestyles.com) in August 2008. Mrs. Hoffmann is also featured on centenarian website adlercentenarians.org, and honors have been presented to her from three southeastern Florida cities.

The author's prior years of documenting family stories, writing some news articles related to positive aging, and even publishing some poetry, were a mere warm-up for the whirlwind Elsa stirred up. As several of these media contacts encouraged Sharon to write more, she made the decision to put it all in book form. She quite naturally took on the task of sharing Elsa's insights to the delight of Elsa's fans, and for all those seeking a "real person" example of positive aging and living.

Holding a B.A. in English from Rutgers College of Rutgers University, New Brunswick, Sharon was well-prepared to use the skills learned from there. In addition, she is a Baby Boomer who can easily incorporate how Elsa's philosophies can help this age group in addition to Seniors.

Sharon worked for almost 20 years in large corporations in the NY and NJ area, but she also held sales jobs in such diverse places as a spa and water park/ski resort. Although some of her corporate jobs were quite fulfilling, such as a Service Specialist at Merrill Lynch in NJ and as part of the Northeast Distribution Center Management Team at Baxter Healthcare in NY, Sharon is most happy now owning and operating a business with her husband Mike in South Florida.

Concentrating on career first, from college graduation through most of her thirties, is something many Boomers can relate to. Sharon did not marry until her late 30's. At 40, she and her husband Mike started a new business from scratch. At 44, Sharon and Mike adopted two beautiful little girls. She has not let her age deter her from plans others may see as reserved for those years younger. One can see how Elsa's extraordinary example has definitely enhanced Sharon's life in big ways.

This famous quote, often misattributed to Emerson, answers what success is; It has always made Elsa's granddaughter Sharon think of Elsa. It was written in 1904 by Bessie Stanley. Even though it's written in past tense, the words describe to Sharon how Elsa is and has always been:

"He has achieved success who has lived well, laughed often and loved much; who has gained the respect of intelligent men and the love of little children; who has filled his niche and accomplished his task; who has left the world better than he found it, whether by an improved poppy, a perfect poem, or a rescued soul; who has never lacked appreciation of earth's beauty or failed to express it; who has always looked for the best in others and given them the best he had; whose life was an inspiration; whose memory a benediction."

www.elsasownbluezone.com

BUY A SHARE OF THE FUTURE IN YOUR COMMUNITY

These certificates make great holiday, graduation and birthday gifts that can be personalized with the recipient's name. The cost of one S.H.A.R.E. or one square foot is $54.17. The personalized certificate is suitable for framing and will state the number of shares purchased and the amount of each share, as well as the recipient's name. The home that you participate in "building" will last for many years and will continue to grow in value.

Here is a sample SHARE certificate:

THIS CERTIFIES THAT

YOUR NAME HERE

HAS INVESTED IN A HOME FOR A DESERVING FAMILY

1985-2005

TWENTY YEARS OF BUILDING FUTURES IN OUR
COMMUNITY ONE HOME AT A TIME

1200 SQUARE FOOT HOUSE @ $65,000 = $54.17 PER SQUARE FOOT
This certificate represents a tax deductible donation. It has no cash value.

YES, I WOULD LIKE TO HELP!

I support the work that Habitat for Humanity does and I want to be part of the excitement! As a donor, I will receive periodic updates on your construction activities but, more importantly, I know my gift will help a family in our community realize the dream of homeownership. **I would like to SHARE in your efforts against substandard housing in my community!** *(Please print below)*

PLEASE SEND ME _____ SHARES at $54.17 EACH = $ $_____

In Honor Of: _____

Occasion: (Circle One)   HOLIDAY   BIRTHDAY   ANNIVERSARY

     OTHER: _____

Address of Recipient: _____

Gift From: _____ *Donor Address:* _____

Donor Email: _____

I AM ENCLOSING A CHECK FOR $ $_____ PAYABLE TO HABITAT FOR HUMANITY OR PLEASE CHARGE MY VISA OR MASTERCARD *(CIRCLE ONE)*

Card Number _____ Expiration Date: _____

Name as it appears on Credit Card _____ Charge Amount $ _____

Signature _____

Billing Address _____

Telephone # Day _____ Eve _____

PLEASE NOTE: Your contribution is tax-deductible to the fullest extent allowed by law.
Habitat for Humanity • P.O. Box 1443 • Newport News, VA 23601 • 757-596-5553
www.HelpHabitatforHumanity.org

CPSIA information can be obtained
at www.ICGtesting.com
Printed in the USA
JSHW021352140123
36290JS00001B/85